Can I Afford Retirement?

An Easy-to-Understand
Source and Planning Book

J.G. Krane

New Leaf Communication
San Juan Capistrano, California

Published by:

New Leaf Communication
P.O. Box 101
San Juan Capistrano, CA 92693

Copyright © J.G. Krane, 1993

Library of Congress Cataloging in publication Data
Krane, J.G.
Can I Afford Retirement?: An Easy-to-Understand
Source and Planning Book.

CIP 92-64282   ISBN 0-9633581-0-3: $19.95 Softcover

FOREWORD

The picture many of us carry in our minds is this: we retire to our safe haven to enjoy peace, tranquility, our pension, grandchildren, unlimited time off and, at last, the chance to do all those things we put off 'till now. Is this picture likely to materialize for most of us? As Mr. Krane points out so ably in this fine, new book, not unless we do a number of things. What are these things? This is the sum and substance of his book...explained in clear, readable text, this book is a must read for anyone smart enough to contemplate and plan for retirement early on in their career. It is equally essential for those of us who may have waited too long. In other words, it is never too late to obtain the important information provided by the author. Taking his many good suggestions to heart, doing the necessary work, preparing yourself and your family for the future will all help you achieve the picture of retirement you have carried in your mind.

Topics include: social security, relocating, legal aspects, safety, protection, health, new careers and extensive coverage of multiple resources available to those contemplating retiring. A very useful self-analysis questionnaire is provided, complete with instructions on how to interpret its results and conclusions. This book is obviously the result of extensive research on the part of the author, to whom we owe a debt of gratitude.

David L. Austin, Ph.D.

David L. Austin is the president of the La Jolla Institute for Excellence. He has a Bachelors and Masters degree in Social Science, and a Doctorate in Organizational Psychology. He has held senior-level Human Resource positions in a variety of companies, including Control Data, MA/COM Linkabit, and the Eastman Kodak Company. He is a widely published author in the field of Human Resource Management. On the faculty of three leading Universities and he has lectured on a wide variety of Management topics including retirement issues.

CONTENTS

CHAPTER 1

Introduction

CHAPTER 1

Introduction

Retirement has many definitions to many people. It means no work, lots of idle time, and conjures up many negative images of ending an active life. We regard retired population as out of the mainstream, people with sweaters walking aimlessly through our cities and villages or sitting on park benches, feeding the pigeons. Even the American Heritage Dictionary describes retirement in part as "seclusion or privacy, a retreat." The word "old" is associated with retirement.

But getting older is a process that occurs by itself. It is a process that continues no matter what we do. But it is what *we* do with age that is important. Just who is old anyway? A 40 year old baseball player, a 50 year old military person, a 55 year old retired auto worker or a 70 year old farmer? In most cases these people are not ready for a rocking chair or leisure life. Most people who reach the retirement age are likely to continue with an active life. It is not a question of how old you are, it is a question of: "are you *ready* to retire?" It is even more important: can I afford to retire. We often say, "If I win the lottery I'll retire." Do not be too sure. If you work hard and regularly for years you are likely to find yourself completely unhappy when you retire unless you have prepared yourself for retirement. If food and shelter are provided, we can certainly live without work, but the difference between that and a happy retirement lies in one's state of mind. Isn't it odd that even people who have dreamed of retirement for years, and who can finally retire voluntarily, need an excuse to stop work and enjoy life. Planning to be happy without work seems troublesome. We all have been taught to believe in the goodness of work. "It is noble to work," "The devil finds work for idle hands," "Do your chores first, then you can play," "Business comes before pleasure." We accept work as a natural act. We also distinguish between good work and questionable work, work which is long, hard, and painstaking and work which is easy, quick, and ambiguous. The hard way seems virtuous. A television commercial tells us about "earning money the old fashioned way."

In almost all societies the kind of work a person does is an important factor in establishing his or her position and status. When we retire and give up our work we may lose this status. As a community we look up to some positions. Even the clothes we wear identifies us by the type of work we do. Judges have robes; cooks wear white hats; police wear uniforms and badges; pilots wear uniforms with insignias that indicate their ranks. We have white collar workers and blue collar workers. We are dependent upon the status and respect which our work earns for us. The honor and dignity of our work supports our self respect. But retirement is a leveling process. It is important to identify those aspects in preparing for retirement.

Retirement is also a new beginning; it means independence, new expectations; it is an American dream suddenly come true. Planning for retirement is essential. It can also be an exciting part of your life.

Planning your retirement at 62 or 65 is often too late. Start as early as 5 to 10 years prior to your retirement. Planning for retirement is possibly the largest task of your life. Establish a check list that includes:

1. What will I do during my retirement?
2. What about my financial situation?
3. What about Social Security?
4. What about my health insurance?
5. Do I want to move to another community?

Also be sure to *add your own questions* about your retirement.

Your retirement years count for almost one-fourth of your life time. Most insurance companies tell us that people who retire at 60 can expect to live another 20 years. That is 25% of your life, certainly worth planning for. So, set goals *now*. You can do a great deal today to ensure your retirement years to be exciting and wonderful.

It does not matter if you are 40, 50 or 60 years old, determine what you can afford for the retirement lifestyle you seek. Strive for a better lifestyle in the "best years of your life." This book will help guide and prepare you for your new frontier. It is not possible to plan for all possibilities, but let's try to prepare for the major challenges. This book will explore your new life, maybe new career, your income, your health, moving or staying where you are and most of all help give you a positive outlook on retirement.

CHAPTER 2

Some Interesting Statistics

CHAPTER 2

Some Interesting Statistics

Let's review some statistics provided by the government. They found significant changes since the year 1900 in the USA and abroad. The report stated that this century is witnessing unprecedented demographic and technological changes in American society.

There have been significant gains in life expectancy, both at birth and at the older ages. Declining fertility rates have "aged" the U.S. population, and there have been major improvements in health.

By 1980, for the first time in the history of the United States, 50 percent of all Americans were over 30. Today there are many more persons over 65 than there are teenagers. The elderly population has grown from 4.0 percent of the total in 1900 to more than 11.5 percent in 1983. The number of those over 65 is projected to grow from today's 27 million to an estimated 39.3 million by 2010, when they will constitute almost 14 percent of the nation's population.

More significantly, between 2010 and 2020, the older population is expected to increase by more than 12 million, when the first wave of the baby boomers become the elderly of the future. By 2025, there will be more than twice as many older Americans as teenagers (See Fig. 1). These demographic trends are due in large part to technological changes since 1900—changes whose pace is accelerating. This technological revolution has major implications for all aspects of society.

During this century, improved technologies have increased life expectancy at birth from an average of 47 years in 1900 to more than 74 years in 1982. These technological improvements include advances in public hygiene and sanitation, reductions in the prevalence of infectious diseases through immunization and antibiotics, and the continued improvement and accessibility of general health care to all persons. The effects of these advances have been most noticeable at the earliest ages, where dramatic improvements have increased the probability of surviving beyond the first year of life. **Almost four-fifths of all babies born this year can expect to live to age 65; only two-fifths of babies born in 1900 could have expected to live that long.**

Technological advances have also helped reduce mortality rates among the older age groups. During the past 15 years, sharp reductions in death rates from two major killers—heart disease and stroke—have caused mortality rates among the elderly to plummet. Death rates fell more sharply during this period than during any other 15-year period in U.S. history. **More than half of the improvement in life expectancy for the elderly since 1950 has occurred in the past decade.** Recent age-specific mortality rates indicate that this accelerating pace of improvement in life expectancy at older ages will continue for the foreseeable future. The most dramatic changes are the increases in the proportions of people surviving to the oldest ages (i.e., 75 or 85 years). New technologies may lead to changes in the aging of cells that could have consequences for the human life span.

Women Outlive Men in Virtually All Countries

In every developed society, women, on average, live longer than men (Fig. 2). This female advantage exceeds 7 years in North America and several European countries, while most other developed nations have female/male differences of 5 to 7 years. Gains in life expectancy at birth vary by gender have been widening in developed countries for several decades. While current data suggest the possibility of a leveling off or reversal of this trend, it is too early to tell if the difference between male and female life expectancy will in fact narrow. Differences in life expectancy by sex are usually smaller in developing than in developed nations.

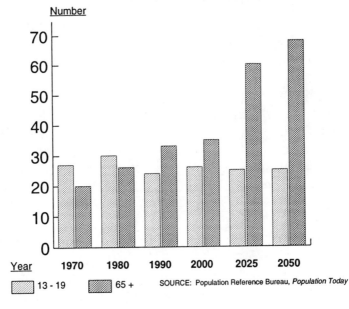

Figure 1.–Number of Teenagers (Aged 13 to 19) and Older Persons (Aged 65 and Over), United States, 1970-2050 (number in millions)

SOURCE: Population Reference Bureau, *Population Today*

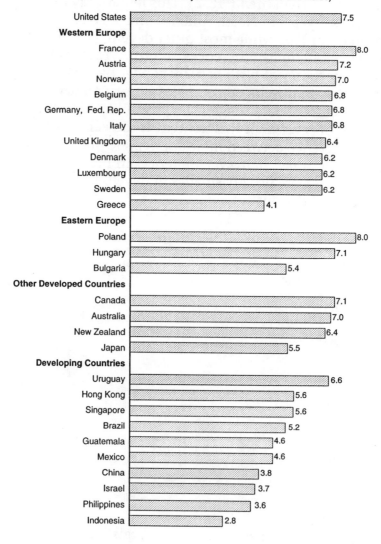

Figure 2
**Female Advantage on
Life Expectancy at Birth: 1985**
(Difference in years between females and males)

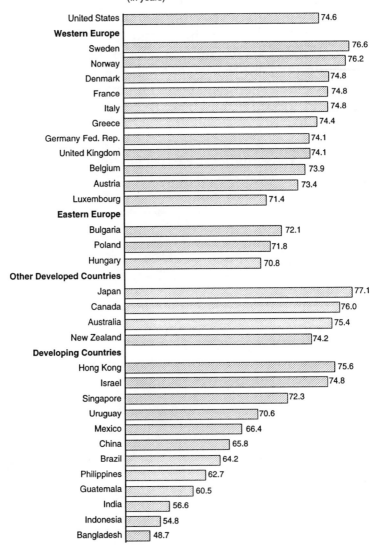

Figure 3
Life Expectancy at Birth: 1985
(In years)

United States	74.6
Western Europe	
Sweden	76.6
Norway	76.2
Denmark	74.8
France	74.8
Italy	74.8
Greece	74.4
Germany Fed. Rep.	74.1
United Kingdom	74.1
Belgium	73.9
Austria	73.4
Luxembourg	71.4
Eastern Europe	
Bulgaria	72.1
Poland	71.8
Hungary	70.8
Other Developed Countries	
Japan	77.1
Canada	76.0
Australia	75.4
New Zealand	74.2
Developing Countries	
Hong Kong	75.6
Israel	74.8
Singapore	72.3
Uruguay	70.6
Mexico	66.4
China	65.8
Brazil	64.2
Philippines	62.7
Guatemala	60.5
India	56.6
Indonesia	54.8
Bangladesh	48.7

Life Expectancy

Expanded health programs have made an enormous difference in developing countries since World War II. Since 1950, the gain in life expectancy in developing regions has been at least as great as the gain during the entire previous half century. The gap in average life expectancy between developed and developing countries had been reduced to about 17 years by 1980.

Among the 31 study countries, several developing nations have higher life expectancies than do some European nations. (Fig. 3).

Conclusion

It is clear that a major challenge into the 21st century will be the maintenance of health and functional ability of the retired population. The world's elderly population currently is growing at a rate of 2.4 percent per year which is much faster than the global population as a whole. This growth rate will result in more than 410 million elderly worldwide by the year of 2000, compared with 290 million today. This number of elderly is expected to continue growing rapidly far into the 21st century (Fig. 4).

Figure 4

Projections of Elderly Population, by Age: 1985 to 2025

■ 80 years and over
▨ 75 years and over
▢ 65 years and over

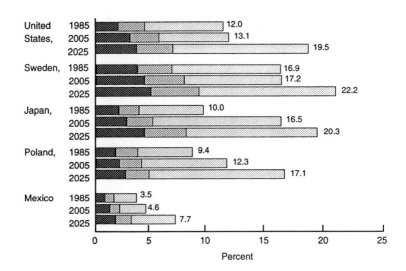

Percent

CHAPTER 3

Retirement Readiness

- Basic Planning
- Self Test
- Financials
- Conclusion

CHAPTER 3

A country squire directed his gardener to plant a seedling of a fruit tree he especially admired, and to get the job done that afternoon. The gardener, knowing his employer was over eighty, pointed out that the tree would not reach its fruit-bearing stage for at least ten years.
"In that case," the country squire said, "Plant it this morning."

Basic Planning

It is essential to know what you need to have when you retire—to be ready and prepared mentally and financially to get retirement off to a happy start. Become "retirement minded" way ahead of time. Planning to be happy without hard work seems wicked. For most of us, laziness has always been a sin, and to be deliberately lazy for the rest of our lives is unthinkable. So, plan a voluntary retirement and become "retirement minded." Set a date, or at least a year, for your retirement. By thinking and planning ahead you will be prepared for your new and exciting retirement lifestyle.

No one can give you an exact estimate of what income you will need for a happy retirement. The amount you will need depends on your taste. Your total expenses in retirement should be no more than 65 to 75 percent of your present day living expenses. It depends on how much golf you play and how much you are going to spend on travel, restaurants, theaters, clothes, etc. The place you expect to live when you retire can make a tremendous difference in the money you will require. Service costs will vary and so will such items as your auto and fire insurance. You must add the cost of climate to your budget too, a light overcoat and a heavy overcoat cost more than no overcoat.

Your retirement budget plan should be flexible. You may want to change it from time to time. You may discover that, over time, certain expenses are not as costly as you anticipated, while others have become higher. A realistic time to start planning for your retirement is about 5 to 10 years prior to actual retirement, the sooner the better. An early start gives you more flexibility. A plan should always include your wants and needs. Your needs need to be met, it is part of contentment and contentment is happiness. Pursuing your wants keeps you active, alert. It is the catalyst for every new day. Getting older is a natural process, it occurs in spite of what we do or eat, but meaningful aging is a human task and it requires an active interest in yourself.

Over the years numerous flyers and brochures came in the mail dealing with retirement issues, with insurance, savings, retirement communities, and the like. But emotionally you were not ready for it because retiring is what you do when you are older, so, consequently you discard all that information. Early planning makes the decision easier because your plan is dictated by an agenda that will prepare you for a successful start. Since it is an important decision, it is a good idea to let your family in on it. In addition to questions you have about retirement your family might have additional questions that have not occurred to you. The need for family participation in the decision of your retirement is crucial because during your retirement you will have the support of your family.

Be prepared and take ample time to plan, mentally and financially. "Retirement readiness" is a condition which needs to be cultivated for many years before you finally enjoy your well deserved time at leisure.

Self Test

Your attitude is as important as your bank account or your pension when it comes to "retirement readiness." Retirement is a major event and doing it involves maybe the hardest decisions you have to make in your life. "Retirement readiness" requires self-study, looking into yourself to determine your readiness for retirement. This is not an easy task, but it is a manageable one. Retirement readiness should contain the elements of being useful. The need to be useful keeps life from being empty and pointless. The active world of work prior to retirement provided most of our usefulness because we produced something, served someone, or created something. Work is great physical and psychological therapy. It kept us physically and mentally alert. The sudden absence of a routine schedule and camaraderie at work can be devastating and have a negative effect on retirement. Work supplies an identity and sense of accomplishment. Remember, those needs need to be filled during retirement years. This is especially true in the early years of retirement; during the transition period into a life of leisure, it is critical.

The following test will help you take a positive step toward new goals and a happy retirement, even if you are not ready to retire. It is a good exercise to prepare you for the best years of your life.

Let's Start With The Test

The questions are straight forward, the test will also put you in the right frame of mind and provide you with information about retirement. The form is simple. For example: question one under "General Questions"—Have you planned your retirement? There are three ways to answer that question. "Yes," if you have indeed made plans toward your retirement. "Somewhat," if you have thought about it and are making some provisions for retirement. "No," if you have not planned at all. Points are assigned to each answer, so that you can rate yourself by the end of the questionnaire. The test will make you think about questions you should ask yourself and facts you should address prior to your retirement. When you have completed page one of "General Questions" you will find on the bottom of the page a space for your total score. Add up the points of each question you have circled and put them in the provided space. Continue with page two and respond to the questions in all categories:

> General Questions
> Health Questions
> Legal Questions
> Financial Questions
> Social Questions

When you are done, and have completed all pages and answered all questions, go to page 36 and enter the total score of each category in the provided space. For instance, enter the total score of "General Questions" (13 questions) in box one under the heading "Total General Questions," then continue and total all individual categories and place the number in provided boxes. When you have completed the five categories, add the scores of all five categories and place that number in space "Total All Questions." Then you are done, so take a rest. The next step is to evaluate yourself. First we will evaluate the total score "Total All Questions." This evaluation will provide you with a general overview of your "retirement readiness." Later we will establish where your weaknesses are, if any.

On page 37 you will see an "Overall Readiness Chart." It is divided into three categories: "Not Prepared," "Need More Preparation," and "Prepared." On the upper part of the chart you will find numbers from 1 through 39. These numbers represent the scores of the test. Take your total score from your test ("Total All Questions") and match it with the number on the chart. You may circle it or write your number below in the open space. If your number falls between 1 through 13, you are not retirement ready. If your number falls between 14 through 32 you are on your way to being retirement ready. If your number falls between 33 through 39 you are considered retirement ready. Remember, this is your overall score. In order to evaluate your strengths and weaknesses we will now test the other categories, health, social, legal, and financial readiness.

In the next pages you will find four additional charts—a Health Readiness Chart, Legal Readiness Chart, Financial Readiness Chart, and a Social Readiness Chart. Again, go back to your scores of your previous test and match the number of your health test with the Health Readiness Chart, exactly as you did with the Overall Readiness Chart. When you have completed the health category proceed with the other categories. After completing all categories you now have a clear view of the results. As you review the scores and your position on the charts you begin to realize what you know about retirement and in what area you have to improve, if any. Study the results and prepare for your retirement. You can and probably should take the test again sometime in the future to reevaluate yourself.

GENERAL QUESTIONS

---

1. Have you planned your retirement?

☐ Yes   3 pts. | ☑ Somewhat   2 pts. | ☐ No   1 pt.

---

2. Do you feel ok about your retirement?

☐ Yes   3 pts. | ☑ Somewhat   2 pts. | ☐ No   1 pt.

---

3. Do you know what to do to feel useful when you retire?

☐ Yes   3 pts. | ☑ Somewhat   2 pts. | ☐ No   1 pt.

---

4. Can you feel useful outside your regular work?

☑ Yes   3 pts. | ☐ Somewhat   2 pts. | ☐ No   1 pt.

---

5. Have you set a date to retire?

☐ Yes   3 pts. | ☑ Somewhat   2 pts. | ☐ No   1 pt.

---

6. Do you look forward to retirement?

☑ Yes   3 pts. | ☑ Somewhat   2 pts. | ☐ No   1 pt.

Total Score This Page _____ Points

13

GENERAL QUESTIONS

---

7. Have you already discussed your retirement with your family and friends?

| ☐ Yes 3 pts. | ☑ Somewhat 2 pts. | ☐ No 1 pt. |

---

8. Have you planned an active or semi-active roll in retirement?

| ☐ Yes 3 pts. | ☑ Somewhat 2 pts. | ☐ No 1 pt. |

---

9. Does your spouse feel ok about retirement? (If married)

| ☐ Yes 3 pts. | ☑ Somewhat 2 pts. | ☐ No 1 pt. |

---

10. Do you consider retirement a major change in your life?

| ☑ Yes 3 pts. | ☐ Somewhat 2 pts. | ☐ No 1 pt. |

---

11. Have you planned a job related activity?

| ☐ Yes 3 pts. | ☑ Somewhat 2 pts. | ☐ No 1 pt. |

Total Score This Page _____ Points

GENERAL QUESTIONS

12. Do you have a hobby?		
☑ Yes 3 pts.	☐ Somewhat 2 pts.	☐ No 1 pt.

13. Have you planned a fun related activity for retirement?		
☑ Yes 3 pts.	☐ Somewhat 2 pts.	☐ No 1 pt.

Total Score This Page _____ Points

17

HEALTH QUESTIONS

1. Will you have health insurance when you retire?		
☐ Yes 3 pts.	☐ Somewhat 2 pts.	☑ No 1 pt.

2. Do you know what your health insurance covers?		
☐ Yes 3 pts.	☐ Somewhat 2 pts.	☑ No 1 pt.

3. Do you know your doctor, hospital, and other medical support centers?		
☑ Yes 3 pts.	☐ Somewhat 2 pts.	☐ No 1 pt.

4. Do you maintain a keen interest in your health?		
☑ Yes 3 pts.	☐ Somewhat 2 pts.	☐ No 1 pt.

5. Do you maintain a healthy diet?		
☑ Yes 3 pts.	☐ Somewhat 2 pts.	☐ No 1 pt.

6. Do you plan to take good care of your health and do you know how to do this?		
☑ Yes 3 pts.	☐ Somewhat 2 pts.	☐ No 1 pt.

Total Score This Page _____ Points

HEALTH QUESTIONS

7. Do you engage in a regular exercise program to maintain fitness?

☐ Yes   3 pts.   ☑ Somewhat   2 pts.   ☐ No   1 pt.

8. Are you familiar with government benefits concerning health?

☐ Yes   3 pts.   ☑ Somewhat   2 pts.   ☐ No   1 pt.

Total Score This Page _____ Points

18

SOCIAL QUESTIONS

1. Do you know what to do when you retire?

☐ Yes   3 pts.   ☑ Somewhat   2 pts.   ☐ No   1 pt.

2. Do you know your community?

☐ Yes   3 pts.   ☑ Somewhat   2 pts.   ☐ No   1 pt.

3. Will you remain in contact with your friends at work after your retirement?

☐ Yes   3 pts.   ☐ Somewhat   2 pts.   ☑ No   1 pt.

4. Do you belong to a church organization, club or other social group?

☑ Yes   3 pts.   ☐ Somewhat   2 pts.   ☐ No   1 pt.

5. Do you plan a social activity on a regular basis?

☐ Yes   3 pts.   ☑ Somewhat   2 pts.   ☐ No   1 pt.

6. Have you considered a support group?

☐ Yes   3 pts.   ☐ Somewhat   2 pts.   ☑ No   1 pt.

Total Score This Page _____ Points

SOCIAL QUESTIONS

7. Have you considered volunteer work in your community?		
☐ Yes 3 pts.	☑ Somewhat 2 pts.	☐ No 1 pt.

8. Have you considered moving to another town when you retire?		
☐ Yes 3 pts.	☐ Somewhat 2 pts.	☑ No 1 pt.

Total Score This Page _____ Points

FINANCIAL QUESTIONS

1. Do you know what your sources of income will be when you retire?

| ☐ Yes   3 pts. | ☑ Somewhat   2 pts. | ☐ No   1 pt. |

2. Have you established a retirement budget?

| ☐ Yes   3 pts. | ☐ Somewhat   2 pts. | ☑ No   1 pt. |

3. Do you know if you will have to work part-time to supplement your retirement income?

| ☐ Yes   3 pts. | ☑ Somewhat   2 pts. | ☐ No   1 pt. |

4. Do you know how much you will receive from Social Security?

| ☑ Yes   3 pts. | ☐ Somewhat   2 pts. | ☐ No   1 pt. |

5. Do you know how much you will receive from your pension, IRA, Keogh, savings, or investments?

| ☐ Yes   3 pts. | ☑ Somewhat   2 pts. | ☐ No   1 pt. |

Total Score This Page _____ Points

FINANCIAL QUESTIONS

---

6. Do you know the Social Security consequences of part
   -time or full-time work?

☐ Yes 3 pts.	☑ Somewhat 2 pts.	☐ No 1 pt.

---

7. Do you have an accountant that can help you when
   needed?

☐ Yes 3 pts.	☑ Somewhat 2 pts.	☐ No 1 pt.

---

8. Do you review your financial position yearly and make
   changes accordingly?

☐ Yes 3 pts.	☑ Somewhat 2 pts.	☐ No 1 pt.

Total Score This Page _____ Points

LEGAL QUESTIONS

1. Do you have a current will or trust established?		
☐ Yes 3 pts.	☑ Somewhat 2 pts.	☐ No 1 pt.

2. Does your spouse have a will or living trust?		
☐ Yes 3 pts.	☑ Somewhat 2 pts.	☐ No 1 pt.

3. Do you know an attorney that can help you when needed?		
☐ Yes 3 pts.	☑ Somewhat 2 pts.	☐ No 1 pt.

4. Do you have a trusted friend or family person you can rely on?		
☑ Yes 3 pts.	☐ Somewhat 2 pts.	☐ No 1 pt.

5. Do you know your pension rights?		
☑ Yes 3 pts.	☐ Somewhat 2 pts.	☐ No 1 pt.

6. Do you know your Social Security rights?		
☐ Yes 3 pts.	☑ Somewhat 2 pts.	☐ No 1 pt.

Total Score This Page _____ Points

14

LEGAL QUESTIONS

> 7. Do you plan to consult your attorney before making a
> substantial gift to relatives, friends or organizations?
>
> ☐ Yes   3 pts. | ☐ Somewhat   2 pts. | ☑ No   1 pt.

> 8. Do you understand the legality of handling the affairs
> of an ill or incompetent person?
>
> ☐ Yes   3 pts. | ☑ Somewhat   2 pts. | ☐ No   1 pt.

Total Score This Page _____ Points

30 **TOTAL GENERAL QUESTIONS**

| _____ Points |

TOTAL HEALTH QUESTIONS

18

| _____ Points |

17 **TOTAL LEGAL QUESTIONS**

| _____ Points |

14 **TOTAL FINANCIAL QUESTIONS**

| _____ Points |

14 **TOTAL SOCIAL QUESTIONS**

| _____ Points |

95 **TOTAL ALL QUESTIONS**

| _____ Points |

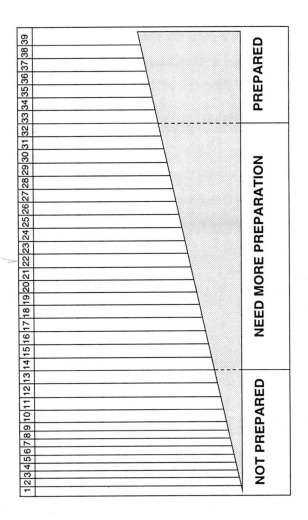

GENERAL READINESS CHART

HEALTH READINESS CHART

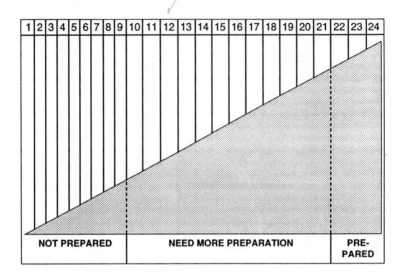

LEGAL READINESS CHART

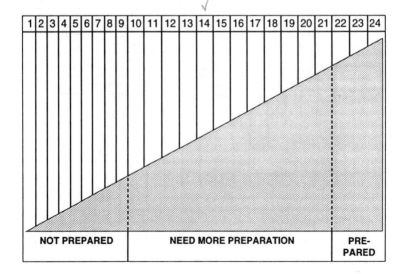

FINANCIAL READINESS CHART

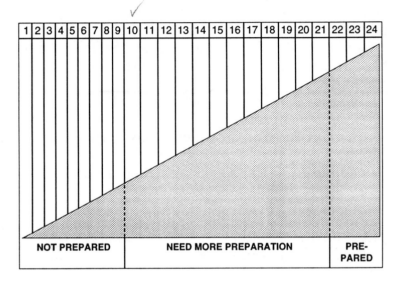

SOCIAL READINESS CHART

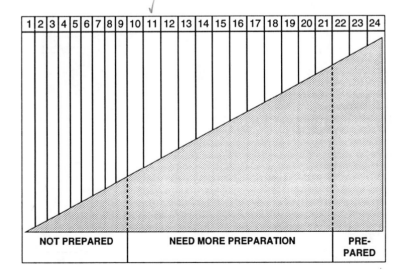

Place the total score, from all categories, on page 36 in appropriate column. If your total score is 110 points place the number in column "B," or if your total score is 126 points place the number in column "A." This readiness chart will indicate your overall readiness.

Group "A" - You are considered to be informed about retirement readiness.

Group "B" - You are on your way to retirement readiness.

Group "C" - You are *not* retirement ready.

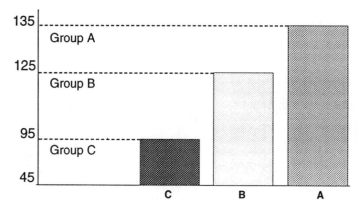

OVERALL READINESS CHART

The Financials

The five categories we have discussed—1) general 2) health, 3) legal, 4) social, and 5) financial are very important to your well-being in your retirement. But we also need a financial plan. We need to know how much money we will need when we retire. By planning ahead you may be able to avoid unpleasant surprises which can cause disappointment and sometimes deep financial troubles. Planning ahead and preparing a financial forecast will provide confidence in your new retirement lifestyle. The financial results may also alter your plans, you may decide to retire earlier or retire later. You may also decide to look for a new job during your retirement. These are important reasons to plan and prepare a financial road map for a secure and happy retirement. Let's get started.

The financial forecast is divided into two parts:

1. Present Financial Status
2. Retirement Financial Forecast

There is good reason for the two parts. You need to establish your present financial position, your current bills, and commitments. After completing the present financial status, compare it with your retirement forecast. This allows you to make plans to adjust payments or eliminate them. For example, you may find, after comparing both financials, that the house payment is satisfactory for today with your present income but it is too high for your income after you retire. So you may have to sell the house and move to a more affordable home. The numbers you enter are current and easy to come by. Sharpen your pencil and start. If you have any questions about the subject, you can refer to page 51 where each entry is explained.

PART 1

Worksheets for Present Financial Status

WORKSHEET FOR PRESENT FINANCIAL STATUS

PRESENT FINANCIAL STATUS			
			Date:_____
	INCOME	PER MONTH	PER YEAR
1.	Salary		
2.	Pension		
3.	Social Security		
4.	Investments		
5.	Other		
6.	Total Income		

BASIC EXPENSES			
7.	House Payment		
8.	Loan Payments		
9.	Insurance		
10.	Taxes		
11.	Other		
12.	Subtotal		

WORKSHEET FOR PRESENT FINANCIAL STATUS

	PRESENT FINANCIAL STATUS		
			Date:_____
	VARIABLE EXPENSES	PER MONTH	PER YEAR
13.	Utilities		
14.	Telephone		
15.	Fuel (Car)		
16.	Food		
17.	Clothing		
18.	Medical		
19.	Heating		
20	Maintenance		
21.	Personal Items		
22.	Other		
23.	Subtotal		

24.	Annual Expenses		
25.	Vacation		
26.	Insurance		
27.	Taxes		
28.	Legal		
29.	Accounting		
30.	Other		
31.	Subtotal		

WORKSHEET FOR PRESENT FINANCIAL STATUS

PRESENT FINANCIAL STATUS			
Totals		Date:	
	EXPENSES	PER MONTH	PER YEAR
32.	Basic Expenses		
33.	Variable Expenses		
34.	Annual Expenses		
35.	Total		

INCOME AND EXPENSE			
		MONTH	YEAR
36.	Income		
37.	Expense		
38.			

PART 2

Worksheets for Retirement Financial Forecast

WORKSHEET FOR PRESENT FINANCIAL STATUS FORECAST

RETIREMENT FINANCIAL STATUS			
			Date:_____
	INCOME	PER MONTH	PER YEAR
1.	Salary		
2.	Pension		
3.	Social Security		
4.	Investments		
5.	Other		
6.	Total Income		

BASIC EXPENSES			
7.	House Payment		
8.	Loan Payments		
9.	Insurance		
10.	Taxes		
11.	Other		
12.	Subtotal		

WORKSHEET FOR PRESENT FINANCIAL STATUS FORECAST

RETIREMENT FINANCIAL STATUS			
			Date:_____
	VARIABLE EXPENSES	PER MONTH	PER YEAR
13.	Utilities		
14.	Telephone		
15.	Fuel (Car)		
16.	Food		
17.	Clothing		
18.	Medical		
19.	Heating		
20	Maintenance		
21.	Personal Items		
22.	Other		
23.	Subtotal		

24.	Annual Expenses		
25.	Vacation		
26.	Insurance		
27.	Taxes		
28.	Legal		
29.	Accounting		
30.	Other		
31.	Subtotal		

WORKSHEET FOR PRESENT FINANCIAL STATUS FORECAST

RETIREMENT FINANCIAL STATUS			
			Date:_____
	EXPENSES	PER MONTH	PER YEAR
32.	Basic Expenses		
33.	Variable Expenses		
34.	Annual Expenses		
35.	Total		

INCOME AND EXPENSE			
		MONTH	YEAR
36.	Income		
37.	Expense		
38.			

Helpful Hints And Explanations
For Your Worksheets

To maintain an accurate history of all your income and expenses, establish a separate sheet of paper for all your details. For example, on income:

Write Down All Sources of Income

Frank:	Ford Motor Comp.	$2,000 per mo.
Alice:	Dr. Johnson's Off.	$1,800 per mo.
Alice:	Avon	$ 200 per mo.
	Total:	$4,000 per mo.

Or on Insurance:

Our Life Insurance	$ 52.50 per mo.
Our Health Insurance	$200.00 per mo.
Homeowners Insurance	$ 35.00 per mo.
Car Insurance	$100.00 per mo.
Total	$387.00 per mo.

This will help you when you need to review your numbers at a later time. You can also change it when life insurance matures or car insurance is paid off. Keep it with your worksheets.

Worksheet Explanations

INCOME

1. All *net* income.

	Example:
Frank: Ford Motor Comp.	$2,000 per mo.
Alice: Dr. Johnson	$1,800 per mo.
Alice: Avon	$ 200 per mo.
Total:	$4,000 per mo.

2. Net income in household.
3. Net income in household.
4. Monthly or yearly income from interest,, stock or bonds, profit sharing, etc.
5. Other income: rental income, etc.
6. Add up all the sources of income to arrive at your total income.

Basic Expenses

Basic expenses are payments you make monthly that do not change from month to month. Like a house payment, mortgage or rent.

7. Include all payments including second home and/or rentals.
8. Include all loan payments, cars, boat, credit cards, second mortgage, etc.
9. Insurance: home, car, health, life, etc.
10. Some taxes, such as property taxes, could be part of your mortgage payment, so make sure not to duplicate your entries. If you pay quarterly taxes divide by 3 and enter 1/3 per month. If you pay yearly taxes enter in yearly column.
11. Enter other basic expenses.
12. Total both per month and yearly column.

Variable Expenses

Variable expenses are expenditures that vary from month to month. Sometimes you spend more on gas from one month to another, or make more phone calls than last month. It is therefore more difficult to provide exact numbers in these columns.

However, nobody can provide better numbers than you can. Look at your phone bills of the last 12 months (or at least the last 6 months) and you will get a clear idea what you have spent on an average per month. Before you establish your average amount make sure that you are on the high end of your estimate. You'll feel better if you have money left over to spend. Do so with all bills that occur on a monthly basis, such as water, gas, medical bills, etc.

13. Utility bills include water, electricity, gas, etc. Combine the numbers and enter the in proper column.
14. Average telephone bill.
15. Fuel and related costs associated with your automobile. Include oil and other cost to maintain your car.
16. Your food bill will take some time to establish the exact monthly cost. Do include supplies like laundry soap, toothpaste, etc.
17. Clothing include all items such as socks, shirts, nylons, shoes, etc.
18. Medical expenses also include prescribed drugs, payments and co-payment on medical bills.
19. Heating on the east coast and the midwest is a significant cost due to the colder weather and should be entered as a single item.
20. Maintenance is a general category but is mainly intended for house maintenance such as paint, plumbing, filters, light bulbs, etc.
21. Personal items include hobbies, sports, theater, movies, etc.

22. Others include public transportation, dues, dry cleaning, beauty shop and costs not men tioned in any other category, such as dining out.
23. Total both monthly and yearly columns.
24. Annual expenses are those that occur on a yearly basis such as property taxes, insurance, etc.
25. Enter vacation expenses. Also add the small vacations, long weekends, etc. that were not entered on previous sheets.
26. Home insurance, or other annual premiums, could be entered here.
27. Enter taxes that are paid annually like property taxes, boat, car, etc. Do not enter them here if you have entered them previously on a monthly basis. Certain taxes are paid monthly and could be part of your mortgage payment.
28. Enter your annual legal costs if any.
29. Enter your annual accounting cost, such as tax preparation fees.
30. Enter all other costs not mentioned above.
31. Total 24 through 31.

Totals

32. Enter the basic expenses subtotal item number 12, per month and per year.
33. Enter the variable expenses subtotal item number 23, per month and per year.
34. Enter the annual expenses subtotal item number 31.
35. Total item 32, 33, and 34 per month and per year.

Income and Expense

   36. Enter item 6, total income per month and per year.

   37. Enter item 35, per month and per year.

Evaluation

The numbers should speak for themselves. The income should be greater than the expense. Item 38 should be a positive number. If it is not, you have to either alter your lifestyle or increase your income. After you have completed your "Present Financial Status" you can now proceed with part two of your financial evaluation: "Retirement Financial Forecast." Remember, this is a forecast, you can alter it at any time in the future. Forecast your income by writing to the Social Security agency. (Read chapter 4 on Social Security.) Ask your employer about your pension income and estimate your interest income, etc. Estimate your basic expenses, variable expenses, annual expenses and complete item 36 and 37.

Conclusion

After completing the questionnaire and evaluating your financial situation, you will begin to realize where you are in respect to retirement readiness. You have answered 135 questions about retirement and spent hours establishing your present financial position and forecasting your financial retirement years. Congratulations. This was hard work but it is the best thing you have done for your retirement preparation. It focuses on some important aspects of your future.

You might want to retire later, or sooner, or you might decide to obtain a part-time job. Not just for additional income but also to provide you with pleasure and to occupy some of your free time. Planning gives you time to identify the kind of industry or direction you would like to work toward. If retirement is ten years away from your retirement you can obviously try to change your financial position a great deal between now and then. A decade before retirement is a good time to take inventory of assets and obligations and make financial choices aimed at maximizing resources. If you feel it is difficult to plan your financial future you may want to seek pre-retirement planning advice from a professional or a community service organization. If you do not have ten years to plan and have one year, or less, to retirement date, "now" is the time to take charge of planning. Indeed, "yesterday" may have been better. *Remember that the numbers and answers to these questions are not cast in stone.* Do not be too hard on yourself. Your plans should be flexible. The main object is to have a comfortable retirement. In terms of your general questionnaire, each question can provoke an uneasiness especially if some of the subjects have never been raised before. Remember they are all important questions and designed to help you discover how you feel about your retirement readiness. When you answer these questions you actually have already begun planning your retirement. When you set a date, you have made a giant step toward a planned retirement.

Your health and social planning are also critical. Because to plan your future you will want to be in good health and spirits to enjoy it. Your social calendar will keep you alert and in charge of living.

The rating of the self test is just an indicator, there are no winners or losers. If you score high marks you will be well on your way to a planned retirement. If you score low, it tells you to start planning *now*. The very reason that you are reading this book indicates that you are already in the planning mode. Once you have developed a program of action, you may discover that it is not complicated and it will add to your confidence level. It makes you feel good about retiring.

The older we are, the more experience we've had with change—in our jobs, our families, even in our bodies. We should be old enough to know, but still young enough to do. As a middle-aged philosopher said: "You feel you have lived long enough to have learned a few things that nobody can learn earlier. That is the reward and that's the excitement. I now see things in books, in people, in music, that I attribute largely to my present age."

Your experience will add to a better tomorrow, and above all a happy retirement.

CHAPTER 4

Your Social Security Benefits
- Disability Benefits
- Benefits For Your Family
- Survivors Benefits
- Supplemental Security Income
- Medicare
- What You Need To Know After You Sign Up For Social Security

CHAPTER 4

Your Social Security Benefits

Social Security will be part of the retirement plans of almost every worker in the United States. The decisions you make about retirement will be some of the most important ones you will ever make. This part of the book provides information you need to know about Social Security benefits to help you plan for your retirement years.

It provides a general overview of Social Security retirement benefits. The information it contains is not intended to cover all provisions of the law. For more information about Social Security and other related benefits contact your local Social Security office. In the last paragraph, "Retirement Resources" you'll find phone numbers and addresses you can contact for specific information.

Before we get started explaining the program, it's important to answer the first question many people have about Social Security. Perhaps you've asked it yourself. That question is: "Will Social Security be there when I need it?" The simple and logical answer is, "Yes it will." But that answer deserves an explanation.

Most of the worries about the future of Social Security result from the financial troubles the system faced in the 1970's and early 1980's. At the time, because of high inflation and other economic problems, Social Security was in very serious financial condition. However, due to an improved economy and increases in Social Security taxes, the system now is in excellent shape—and will be for many years to come.

Social Security takes in significantly more than it spends, and the extra money, called "reserves," make up the Social Security trust funds. There have been reports about so-called "misuse" of those funds. For example, some people complain that Social Security money is used to pay for other government programs. In fact, the money in Social Security's trust funds is invested in Treasury bonds—generally considered the safest of all investments. The Government, by law, has always paid back the trust funds **with interest**, and there is no reason to expect it will not continue to do so.

Beyond the facts and figures that clearly show that Social Security is in excellent financial shape, the program's future is further assured because of the broad support that it enjoys from all sectors of American society. As a nation, we recognize the need to provide a basic level of financial support and health care for the elderly, as well as for the citizens with disabilities, the survivors of deceased workers, and people with low incomes.

That goal is at the heart of our Social Security system. It's what the Retirement, Disability, Survivors Medicare, and Supplemental Security Income (SSI) programs are all about.

When Will You Need Social Security

Now that you know that Social Security will be there when you need it, the next question you may ask yourself is this: "When will I need it?"

If you're like most people, you tend to think of Social Security as a retirement program. Although it's true that most of its beneficiaries (about 60 percent) receive retirement benefits, many others get Social Security:

- Because they are disabled;
- Because they are a dependent of someone who gets Social Security; or
- Because they are a widow, widower, or child of someone who has died.

So, depending on your circumstances, you may be eligible for Social Security at any age. In fact, about 39 million people, almost 1 out of every 6 Americans, collect some kind of Social Security benefit. Those benefits totalled more than **$240 billion** in 1990.

The basic idea behind Social Security is a simple one. You pay taxes into the system during your working years, and you and members of your family receive monthly benefits when you retire or become disabled. Or, your survivors collect benefits when you die.

Here's An Important Point: Social Security is **not** intended to be your only source of income. Instead, it is meant to be used to supplement the pensions, insurance, savings, and other investments you will accumulate during your working years.

The Taxes You Pay

Social Security taxes are used to pay for all Social Security benefits. In addition, a portion of your taxes is used to pay for part of your Medicare coverage. General tax revenues, **not** Social Security taxes, are used to finance the Supplemental Security Income (SSI) program.

If You Work For Someone Else

You **and** your employer pay taxes for Social Security and Medicare. In 1991, you and your employer **each** pay 7.65 percent of your gross salary, up to a limit determined by Congress. In 1991, the limit is $53,400. The deduction might be labelled "FICA" on your pay slip. That stands for Federal Insurance Contributions Act, the law that authorized Social Security's payroll tax.

If You Work For Yourself

If you are self-employed, you pay 15.3 percent of your taxable income into Social Security, up to the same limit of $53,400. However, there are special deductions you can take when you file your tax return that are intended to offset your tax rate.

Extra Taxes For Medicare

If you made more than $53,400 in 1991, you continued to pay the Medicare portion of the Social Security tax up to a limit of $125,000. The Medicare portion of the tax is 1.45 percent for employers and employees each, and 2.9 percent for self-employed people.

You Become Eligible For Social Security By Earning "Credits"

You must work and then pay taxes into Social Security in order to get something out of it. (Of course, some people get benefits as a dependent or survivor on another person's Social Security record.)

As you work and pay taxes, you earn Social Security "credits." Almost everybody who works earns 4 credits per year. To be specific, you earn 1 credit for each $540 in earnings you have—but 4 credits is the maximum that can be earned in 1 year. (The amount of money needed to earn 1 credit goes up every year.)

How many credits you need to qualify for Social Security depends on your age and the kind of benefit you might be eligible for.

Most people need 40 credits (10 years of work) to qualify for benefits. Younger people need fewer credits to be eligible for disability benefits, or for their family members to be eligible for survivors' benefits if they should die.

During your working lifetime, you probably will earn many, many more credits than you need to be eligible for Social Security. The fact that you earn these extra credits does not increase your eventual Social Security benefit. However, the income you earn while working will increase your benefit, as you will learn in the next two sections.

How Much Will You Get From Social Security

The amount of your Social Security benefit is based on factors such as your date of birth, the type of benefit you are applying for, and most important, your earnings.

This book will explain in a general way how a Social Security benefit is figured. But if you would like a detailed and personal estimate of your Social Security retirement, disability, and survivor benefits, all you have to do is call or visit a Social Security office and ask for it.

On page 73 you'll find a copy of the "Request for Earnings and Benefit Estimate Statements." In the last chapter of "Retirement Resources" you will find the address to request this form. Fill out the form and mail it to S.S.I. You should receive your personalized statement in 6 weeks or less.

How Your Benefit Is Figured

In general, a Social Security benefit is based on your earnings averaged over most of your working lifetime. This is different from many private pension plans that are usually based on a relatively small number of years of earnings.

In its simplest terms, here's how your Social Security benefit is figured:

Step 1:   *They determine the number of years of earnings to use as a base.*
Retirement benefits: For everybody born after 1928 and retiring in 1991 or later, which includes most people reading this book, that number is 35 years. Fewer years are used for people born in 1928 or earlier.
Disability and survivors benefits: They use most of the years of earnings posted to your record.

Step 2: *They adjust these earnings for inflation.*

Step 3: *They determine your **average** adjusted earnings based on the number of years figured in step 1.*

Step 4: *They multiply your average adjusted earnings by a percentage that is specified by law.*

That percentage is about 42 percent for people who had average earnings during their working years. The percentage is lower for people in the upper income brackets, and higher for people with low incomes. (That's because the Social Security benefit formula is weighted in favor of low-income workers who have less opportunity to save and invest during their working years.)

How And When To Sign Up For Social Security

You can apply for benefits at any Social Security office. The easiest way to file a claim is to call ahead of time for an appointment. When signing up for retirement, you do so about 3 months before you want your benefits to start.

What Records Will You Need?

To show that you are eligible for Social Security, and to help decide how much your benefits should be, there are certain documents they may ask you to provide. Which ones are necessary depends on the circumstances of your claim.

Here is a list of some of the documents you may need when you sign up for Social Security:

- Your Social Security card (or a record of your number);
- Your birth certificate;
- Children's birth certificates (if they are applying);
- Marriage certificate (if signing up on a spouse's record);
- Your most recent W-2 form, or your tax return if you're self-employed.

This is just a partial list to help you get prepared. When you actually sign up for Social Security, they let you know if other documents are needed.

Direct Deposit

You have a choice of how you receive your Social Security or SSI payments. Your benefit can either be deposited directly into your bank account or come to you in the mail. Most people have their benefits deposited in their bank account because it is safer and more convenient than checks. It is also more efficient.

If you choose direct deposit, have your checkbook or any papers that show your bank account number with you when you sign up for Social Security.

Retirement Benefits

This section of the book provides a brief overview of Social Security retirement benefits. If you

want to learn more about the program, call or visit
your Social Security office.

Full Retirement

If you were born before 1938, you will be eligible
for your full Social Security benefit at the age of 65.

However, beginning in the year 2000, the age at
which full benefits are payable will increase in
gradual steps from 65 to 67. This affects people born
in 1938 and later. For example, if you were born in
1940, your full retirement age is 65 and 6 months. If
you were born in 1950, your full retirement age is 66.
Anybody born in 1960 or later will be eligible for full
retirement benefits at 67.

Reduced Benefits As Early As 62

No matter what your "full" retirement age is,
you may start receiving benefits as early as 62. However, if you start your benefits early, they are reduced
a small percentage for each month before your "full"
retirement age. For example, if your full retirement
age is 65 and you sign up for Social Security when
you're 64, you will receive ninety-three and a third
percent of your full benefit. At 62, you would get 80
percent. (**Note:** The reduction will be greater in
future years as the full retirement age increases.)

Here's An Important Point: There are disadvantages and advantages to taking your benefits before your full retirement age. The disadvantage is that your benefit is permanently reduced. The advantage is that you collect benefits for a longer period of time. Each person's situation is different, so make sure you check with Social Security before you decide to retire.

What About Late Retirement?

Some people continue to work full-time beyond their full retirement age—and they do not sign up for Social Security until later. This delay in retirement can increase your Social Security benefit in two ways:

- Your extra income usually will increase your "average" earnings, which is the basis for determining the amount of your retirement benefit. In other words, the higher your average earnings, the higher your Social Security benefit will be.
- In addition, a special credit is given to people who delay retirement. This credit, which is a percentage added to your Social Security benefit, varies depending on your date of birth. For people turning 65 this year, the rate is 3.5 percent per year. That rate gradually increases in future years, until it reaches 8 percent per year for people turning 65 in 2008 or later.

How Much Will You Get?

We explained how you can get a personalized estimate of the benefits you are due. In addition, there is a chart on page 72 that gives examples of retirement benefit rates.

Examples Of Benefits

Approximate Monthly Benefits If You Retire At Full Retirement Age And Had Steady Lifetime Earnings

Your Age In 1991	Your Family	Your Earnings In 1990			51,300	
		$20,000	$30,000	$40,000	$50,000	Or More[1]
45	You	$ 863	$ 1,124	$ 1,263	$ 1,392	$ 1,422
	You and your spouse[2]	$ 1,294	$ 1,686	$ 1,894	$ 2,088	$ 2,133
55	You	$ 783	$ 1,014	$ 1,106	$ 1,181	$ 1,195
	You and your spouse[2]	$ 1,174	$ 1,521	$ 1,659	$ 1,771	$ 1,792
65	You	$ 725	$ 926	$ 982	$ 1,021	$ 1,022
	You and your spouse[2]	$ 1,087	$ 1,389	$ 1,473	$ 1,531	$ 1,533

[1] Use this column if you earn more than the maximum Social Security earnings base.

[2] Your spouse is assumed to be the same age as you. Your spouse may qualify for a higher retirement benefit based on his or her own work record.

Note: The accuracy of these estimates depends on the pattern of your actual past earnings, and on your earnings in the future.

SOCIAL SECURITY ADMINISTRATION

Request for Earnings and Benefit Estimate Statement

To receive a free statement of your earnings covered by Social Security and your estimated future benefits, all you need to do is fill out this form. Please print or type your answers. When you have completed the form, fold it and mail it to us.

1. Name shown on your Social Security card:

First   Middle Initial   Last

2. Your Social Security number as shown on your card:

☐☐☐ - ☐☐ - ☐☐☐☐

3. Your date of birth:

Month   Day   Year

4. Other Social Security numbers you may have used:

☐☐☐ - ☐☐ - ☐☐☐☐
☐☐☐ - ☐☐ - ☐☐☐☐

5. Your Sex: ☐ Male ☐ Female

6. Other names you have used (including a maiden name):

7. Show your actual earnings for last year and your estimated earnings for this year. Include only wages and/or net self-employment income subject to Social Security tax.

   A. Last year's actual earnings:

   $ ☐☐☐,☐☐☐.☐ 0
   Dollars only

   B. This year's estimated earnings:

   $ ☐☐☐,☐☐☐.☐ 0
   Dollars only

8. Show the age at which you plan to retire: _____

9. Below, show an amount which you think best represents your future average yearly earnings between now and when you plan to retire. The amount should be a yearly average, not your total future lifetime earnings. Only show earnings subject to Social Security tax.

   Most people should enter the same amount as this year's estimated earnings (the amount shown in 7B). The reason for this is that we will show your retirement benefit estimate in today's dollars, but adjusted to account for average wage growth in the national economy.

   However, if you expect to earn significantly more or less in the future than what you currently earn because of promotions, a job change, part-time work, or an absence from the work force, enter the amount in today's dollars that will most closely reflect your future average yearly earnings. Do not add in cost-of-living, performance, or scheduled pay increases or bonuses.

   Your future average yearly earnings:

   $ ☐☐☐,☐☐☐.☐ 0 0
   Dollars only

10. Address where you want us to send the statement:

Name

Street Address (Include Apt. No., P.O. Box, or Rural Route)

City   State   Zip Code

I am asking for information about my own Social Security record or the record of a person I am authorized to represent. I understand that if I deliberately request information under false pretenses I may be guilty of a federal crime and could be fined and/or imprisoned. I authorize you to send the statement of my earnings and benefit estimates to me or my representative through a contractor.

Please sign your name (Do not print)

▲

Date   (Area Code) Daytime Telephone No.

ABOUT THE PRIVACY ACT
Social Security is allowed to collect the facts on this form under Section 205 of the Social Security Act. We need them to quickly identify your record and prepare the earnings statement you asked us for. Giving us these facts is voluntary. However, without them we may not be able to give you an earnings and benefit estimate statement. Neither the Social Security Administration nor its contractor will use the information for any other purpose.   SP

1. Disability Benefits

This section of the book provides a brief overview of Social Security's disability program. It concentrates primarily on benefits for people who have worked and earned enough Social Security "credits" to qualify for disability on their own work record.

However, it is important to note that other kinds of disability benefits are available from Social Security, depending on your circumstances. These include:

- Widows and widowers with disabilities who are eligible for benefits on the record of a spouse;
- People with disabilities who have low income and few assets who might be eligible for SSI benefits;
- Disabled children over age 18 who might be eligible for Social Security benefits on the record of a parent or disabled children at any age who might be eligible for SSI benefits on their own.

What You Should Do If You Become Disabled

If you become disabled, you should file for disability benefits as soon as possible. You can do this by calling or visiting any Social Security office.

You can shorten the time it takes to process your claim if you have the following medical and vocational information when you apply:

- The names, addresses, and phone numbers of your doctors, and of hospitals, clinics, etc., where you have been treated, and
- A summary of where you worked in the last 15 years and the kind of work you did.

Here's An Important Point: You should understand that Social Security's disability rules are different from those of other private plans or government agencies. So the fact that you qualify for disability from somebody else does not mean you will be eligible for Social Security. By the same token, the fact that you have a statement from your doctor indicating you are disabled does not mean you will be automatically eligible for Social Security disability payments.

When Do Your Disability Benefits Start?

If they decide you are disabled, in most cases your monthly benefits will begin effective with the 6th full month of your disability. Here's a simple example of how this works:

John has a severe heart attack on March 15th. He files for disability on March 29th, and his claim is approved on May 30th. September is the 6th full month that he is disabled, so his benefits begin effective that month. Social Security checks are usually paid on the 3rd of the following month, so John's first check (the September check) will arrive October 3rd.

Here's An Important Point: Do not delay signing up for Social Security because of this waiting period. By filing early, all the paperwork will be processed before your first check is due. There is no "waiting period" for disabled children's benefits or for SSI disability payments.

How Much Will You Get?

On page 72, we told you how you can get a personalized estimate of any benefits you are due. In addition, there is a chart on page 78 that gives examples of disability benefit rates.

Worker's Compensation

If you get worker's compensation or certain other government disability benefits, your Social Security disability benefit may be reduced. This is because the law states that the sum of all your disability payments cannot exceed 80 percent of your earnings averaged over a period of time shortly before you became disabled.

How Long Will Your Disability Benefits Continue?

You will continue to get disability benefits unless your condition improves or you return to "substantial" work. They check your claim periodically to determine if this is the case. To help them decide, you may be asked to undergo a special test or examination that they will pay for.

Incentives To Return To Work

There are special rules that help people who would like to return to work but are concerned about the effect this might have on their disability benefits. These rules offer special incentives that permit people to try working without the risk of a sudden loss of their monthly benefits and their Medicare or Medicaid coverage.

Approximate Monthly Benefits If You Become Disabled In 1991 And Had Steady Earnings

Your Age	Your Family	Your Earnings In 1990					
		$10,000	$20,000	$30,000	$40,000	$50,000	$51,300 Or More[1]
25	You	$ 473	$ 732	$ 958	$ 1,079	$ 1,196	$ 1,202
	You, spouse & child[2]	$ 687	$ 1,098	$ 1,437	$ 1,619	$ 1,795	$ 1,803
35	You	$ 468	$ 722	$ 950	$ 1,069	$ 1,174	$ 1,177
	You, spouse & child[2]	$ 674	$ 1,083	$ 1,426	$ 1,604	$ 1,762	$ 1,766
45	You	$ 467	$ 720	$ 947	$ 1,040	$ 1,103	$ 1,105
	You, spouse & child[2]	$ 672	$ 1,081	$ 1,421	$ 1,560	$ 1,655	$ 1,657
55	You	$ 469	$ 724	$ 934	$ 997	$ 1,040	$ 1,041
	You, spouse & child[2]	$ 676	$ 1,086	$ 1,402	$ 1,496	$ 1,561	$ 1,562
64	You	$ 476	$ 736	$ 942	$ 997	$ 1,035	$ 1,036
	You, spouse & child[2]	$ 690	$ 1,104	$ 1,414	$ 1,496	$ 1,553	$ 1,554

[1] Use this column if you earn more than the maximum Social Security earnings base.
[2] Equals the maximum family benefit.

Note: The accuracy of these estimates depends on the pattern of your actual past earnings.

2. Benefits For Your Family

This section of the book provides a brief overview of benefits payable to members of your family when you are eligible for retirement or disability benefits.

Who Can Get Benefits?

When you start collecting Social Security retirement or disability benefits, other members of your family might also be eligible for payment. For example, benefits can be paid to:

- Your husband or wife if he or she is 62 or older (unless he or she collects a higher Social Security benefit on his or her own record);
- Your husband or wife at any age if he or she is caring for your child (the child must be under 16 or disabled);
- Your children, if they are unmarried and:
  —Under 18; or
  —Under 19 but in elementary or secondary school as a full-time student; or
  —Over 18 but severely disabled (the disability must have started before age 22).

How Much Can Family Members Get?

Usually, a family member will be eligible for a benefit equal to 50 percent of your retirement or disability rate. Your spouse is eligible for the 50 percent rate if he or she is 65 or older **or** if he or she is caring for your minor or disabled child. If your spouse is under 65 and does not have a minor or disabled child, the rate is reduced a small percentage for each month before age 65. The lowest the rate can go is 37.5 percent at 62.

Maximum Family Benefits

There is a limit to the amount of money that can be paid on each Social Security record. The limit varies, but is generally equal to about 150 to 180 percent of your benefit rate. If the sum of the benefits payable on your account is greater than this family limit, then the benefits to the family members will be reduced proportionately. Your benefit will **not** be affected.

Benefits For Divorced People

If you are divorced (even if you have remarried), your ex-spouse can be eligible for benefits on your record. In some situations, he or she could get benefits even if you're not receiving them. In order to qualify, your ex-spouse must:

- Have been married to you for at least 10 years;
- Be a least 62 years old;
- Not be eligible for an equal or higher benefit on his or her own Social Security record, or on someone else's Social Security record.

Here's An Important Point: If your ex-spouse receives benefits on your account, it does not affect the amount of any benefits payable to you or your other family members.

3. Survivors Benefits

This section of the book provides a brief overview of the benefits payable when a family breadwinner dies. For more information, call or visit your Social Security office.

Who Can Receive Survivors Benefits?

When you die, certain members of your family may be eligible for benefits on your Social Security record if you had earned enough credits while you were working.

The family members who can collect benefits include:

- A widow or widower who is 60 or older;
- A widow or widower who is 50 or older and disabled;
- A widow or widower at any age if she or he is caring for a child under 16 or a disabled child;
- Children if they are unmarried and:
  —Under 18; or
  —Under 19 but in an elementary or secondary school as a full-time student; or
  —Over 18 but severely disabled (the disability must have started before age 22);

- Your parents, if they were dependent on you for most of their support.

Special One-Time Death Benefit

If you had enough credits, a special one-time payment of $255 also will be made. This payment can only be paid to certain members of your family.

Benefits To Divorced Widows and Widowers

If you are divorced (even if you have remarried), your ex-spouse will be eligible for benefits on your record when you die. In order to qualify, your ex-spouse must:

- Be at least 60 years old (or 50 if disabled) and have been married to you for at least 10 years;
- Be any age if caring for a child who is eligible for benefits on your record.
- Not be eligible for an equal or higher benefit on his or her own record;
- Not be currently married, unless the remarriage occurred after 60—or 50 for disabled widows. (In cases of remarriage after the age of 60, your ex-spouse will be eligible for a widow's benefit on your record, or a dependent's benefit on the record of his or her new spouse, whichever is higher.)

Here's An Important Point: If your ex-spouse receives benefits on your account, it does not affect the amount of benefits payable to other survivors on your record.

How Much Will Your Survivors Get?

The amount payable to your survivors is a percentage of your basic Social Security benefit—usually in a range from 75 percent to 100 percent.

The Personal Earnings and Benefit Estimate Statement, explained on page 66 will provide you with a more accurate measurement of potential survivors benefits payable on your record. In addition, there is a chart on page 84 that gives examples of survivors benefit rates.

Maximum Family Benefits

Like payments to your family members if you are retired or disabled, there is a limit to the amount of money that can be paid each month to your survivors. The limit varies, but is generally equal to about 150 to 180 percent of your benefit rate. If the sum of the benefits payable to your surviving family members is greater than this limit, then the benefits to your family will be reduced proportionately.

The chart below gives examples of benefits that can be paid in different situations.

Approximate monthly Survivors Benefits If The Worker Dies In 1991 And Had Steady Earnings

Worker's Age	Worker's Family	Deceased Worker's Earnings In 1990				
		$20,000	$30,000	$40,000	$50,000	$51,300 Or More[1]
35	Spouse and 1 child[2]	$1,090	$1,430	$1,610	$1,784	$1,790
	Spouse and 2 children[3]	$1,338	$1,668	$1,879	$2,082	$2,088
	1 child only	$545	$715	$805	$892	$895
	Spouse at age 60[4]	$519	$682	$768	$850	$853
45	Spouse and 1 child[2]	$1,082	$1,422	$1,566	$1,668	$1,670
	Spouse and 2 children[3]	$1,330	$1,658	$1,828	$1,945	$1,948
	1 child only	$541	$711	$783	$834	$835
	Spouse at age 60[4]	$515	$678	$747	$795	$796
55	Spouse and 1 child[2]	$1,086	$1,402	$1,496	$1,560	$1,562
	Spouse and 2 children[3]	$1,334	$1,635	$1,745	$1,820	$1,822
	1 child only	$543	$701	$748	$780	$781
	Spouse at age 60[4]	$517	$668	$713	$744	$744

[1] Use this column if the worker earned more than the maximum Social Security earnings base.
[2] Amounts shown also equal the benefits paid to two children, if no parent survives or surviving parent has substantial earnings.
[3] Equals the maximum family benefit.
[4] Amounts payable in 1991. Spouses turning 60 in the future would receive higher benefits.
Note: The accuracy of these estimates depends on the pattern of the worker's actual earnings in prior years.

4. Supplemental Security Income

This section of the book provides a brief overview of the Supplemental Security Income program. For more information, call or visit Social Security to ask for a free copy of the booklet, *Supplemental Security Income.*

What Is Supplemental Security Income?

Supplemental Security Income is usually called "SSI" for short. Although this program is run by Social Security, the money to pay for SSI benefits does not come from Social Security taxes or Social Security trust funds of the U.S. Treasury.

SSI makes monthly payments to people who have low incomes and few assets. In addition, to get SSI you must:

- Be living in the U.S. or the Northern Mariana Islands;
- Be a U.S. citizen or be living in the U.S. legally;

And you must be:
- 65 or older; or
- Blind, or
- Disabled.

Here's An Important Point: Children as well as adults can get SSI benefits because of blindness or disability.

What Are The Income And Asset Limits?

To get SSI, your income and the value of the things you own must be below certain limits.

Income

By the term "income," they mean the money you have coming in such as earnings, Social Security, or other government checks, pension, etc. But they also mean "non-cash" items you receive such as the value of free food and shelter.

How much income you can have and still get SSI depends on whether you work or not—and in which State you live.

If you don't work, you may be able to get SSI if your monthly income adds up to less than:

- $427 for one person; or
- $630 for a couple.

If you do work, you can have more income each month and still get SSI. If all of your income is from working, you may be able to get SSI if you make less than:

- $899 a month for one person, or
- $1,305 a month for a couple.

Here's An Important Point: Some States have higher SSI rates (and, therefore, higher income limits) than others. The limits mentioned above are the minimum Federal rates. Check with your local Social Security office to find out if your State has higher SSI rates and income limits.

Assets

Assets are the things you own.

But they don't count everything you own when they decide if you can get SSI. For example, they don't count your home and many of your personal belongings, and they usually don't count your car. But they do count assets like cash and bank accounts.

You may be able to get SSI if the things you own that count are not more than:

- $2,000 for one person; or
- $3,000 for a couple.

Unlike the income category, these limits do not change from State to State.

How Much Can You Get From SSI?

The basic monthly SSI check is the same in all States. In 1991, the basic rate is:

- $407 for one person;
- $610 for a couple.

But some States add money to the basic rate, so you may get more if you live in one of these States.

The basic rate is less if you live rent-free in somebody else's home, or if you live in an institution where your room and board is paid for by the State.

SSI For People With Disabilities—Including Children

As indicated earlier, people with disabilities, including children, can get SSI.

Most of the rules used to decide if a person has condition severe enough to qualify for Social Security disability benefits also apply to SSI.

And as with Social Security, the SSI program has special plans designed to help people who want to try going back to work without the risk of suddenly losing their benefits or Medicaid coverage.

Here's An Important Point: Social Security has recently developed new standards for evaluating disability in children. These new rules are expected to mean that more children may qualify for SSI. If you have a child with a disability who was previously denied for SSI, you should contact your local Social Security office to re-apply under the new standards.

Other Help You Can Get

Most people who get SSI can also get food stamps and "Medicaid" assistance. Medicaid, which is a different program than Medicare, helps pay doctor and hospital bills.

5. Medicare

Medicare is our country's basic health insurance program for people 65 or older and for many disabled people.

You should not confuse Medicare and Medicaid. Medicaid is a health insurance program for people with low income and limited assets. It is usually run by state welfare or human service agencies. Some people qualify for one or the other, some qualify for both Medicare and Medicaid.

This book provides only a brief overview of the Medicare program. If you would like to learn more about Medicare, call or visit your Social Security office.

Medicare Has Two Parts

There are two parts to Medicare:

- Hospital insurance (sometimes called "Part A")—This helps pay for inpatient hospital care and certain follow-up services; and
- Medical insurance (sometimes called "Part B")—This helps pay for doctors' services, outpatient hospital care, and other medical services.

Who Is Eligible For Hospital Insurance (Part A)?

Most people get hospital insurance when they turn 65. You qualify for it automatically if you are eligible for Social Security or Railroad Retirement benefits. Or you may qualify on a spouse's (including divorced spouse's) record. Others qualify because they are government employees not covered by Social Security who paid the Medicare part of the Social Security tax.

In addition, if you have been getting Social Security disability benefits for 24 months, you will qualify for hospital insurance.

Also, people who have permanent kidney failure that requires maintenance dialysis or a kidney replacement qualify for hospital insurance if they are insured, or the spouse or child of an insured worker.

Almost everybody qualifies for hospital insurance through one of the above methods. But if you don't, and if you're 65 or older, you can buy hospital insurance just like you can buy other health insurance policies.

Who Can Get Medical Insurance (Part B)?

Almost anyone who is eligible for hospital insurance can sign up for medical insurance. Unlike Part A, which was paid for by your taxes while you worked and is free when you're eligible for it, Part B is an optional program that costs $29.90 per month. Almost everybody signs up for this part of Medicare.

How Do You Get Medicare?

If you are already getting Social Security benefits when you turn 65, you will be automatically enrolled in Medicare (although you have the opportunity to turn down "Part B").

If you are disabled, you will be automatically enrolled in Medicare after you have been getting disability benefits for 24 months. (And you can turn down "Part B" if you want.)

If you turn 65 but plan to keep working and do not plan to sign up for Social Security at that time, you should call or visit a Social Security office so they can help you decide if you should sign up for Medicare only.

There are many other rules associated with Medicare enrollment. Please contact your Social Security office for more details.

What Does Medicare Pay For?

Medicare hospital insurance helps pay for:

- Inpatient hospital care;
- Skilled nursing facility care;
- Home health care;
- Hospice care.

Medicare medical insurance helps pay for:

- Doctor's services;
- Outpatient hospital services;
- Home health visits;
- Diagnostic x-ray, laboratory, and other tests;
- Necessary ambulance services; and
- Other medical services and supplies.

What Medicare Does Not Pay For

Not all health services are covered by Medicare. For example, Medicare does **not** pay for:

- Custodial care;
- Dentures and routine dental care;
- Eyeglasses, hearing aids, and examinations to prescribe and fit them;
- Nursing home care (except skilled nursing care);
- Prescription drugs; and
- Routine physical checkups and related tests.

6. What You Need To Know After You Sign Up For Social Security

After you've signed up for retirement, disability, survivors, Medicare, or SSI benefits, your involvement with Social Security is just beginning. This section of the book provides a brief overview of a few things you need to know about your benefits and how they work.

When you start getting Social Security, they send you a booklet that explains your rights and responsibilities. In addition, they produce a variety of publications that explain other facts you need to know about Social Security and SSI. **If you need more information**, call or visit Social Security to tell them your situation. There is probably a pamphlet or fact sheet they can send you that will answer your questions.

What You Need To Report

People who get Social Security should let them know when something happens that might affect their benefits. Here are some examples:

- If they move;
- If they get married or divorced;
- If their name changes;
- If their income or earnings change;
- If a child is born or adopted;
- If a beneficiary is imprisoned;
- If they leave the United States;
- If a beneficiary dies.

If You Disagree With A Decision

Whenever they make a decision that affects your eligibility for Social Security or SSI benefits, they send you a letter that explains their decision. If you disagree with the decision, you have the right to appeal it. In other words, you can ask them to review your case. If their decision was wrong, they will change it.

There are several levels of appeal that are available within the Social Security system. Beyond that, you can take your case to a Federal court.

If you would like to learn more about these other steps, and about the appeals process in general, call or visit any Social Security office to ask for a copy of the fact sheet called *The Appeals Process*.

How Your Earnings Affect Your Benefits

There is a provision in the law that limits the amount of money you can earn and still collect all your Social Security benefits. This provision affects people under the age of 70 who collect Social Security retirement, dependents, or survivors benefits. (People 70 or older have no restrictions on their outside earnings. People who work and collect disability or SSI benefits have different earnings requirements and should report all their income to Social Security.)

If you are under age 65, you can earn up to $7,080 in 1991 and still collect all your Social Security benefits.

However, for every $2 you earn over this limit, $1 will be withheld from your Social Security benefits.

If you are age 65 through 69, you can earn up to $9,720 in 1991 and still collect all your Social Security benefits.

However, for every $3 you earn over this limit, $1 will be withheld from your Social Security benefits.

They only count the earnings you make from a job or your net profit if you're self-employed. This includes compensation such as bonuses, commissions, and vacation pay. It does **not** include such items as pensions, annuities, investment income, interest, Social Security, veterans, or other government benefits.

If you would like to learn more about the Social Security earnings limits and how they affect you, call or visit any Social Security office to ask for a free copy of the fact sheet, *How Work Affects Your Social Security Benefits.*

Your Benefits May Be Taxable

A relatively small number of people who get Social Security will have to pay taxes on their benefits. This provision only affects people in the higher income tax brackets.

If you file a Federal tax return as an "individual," you might have to pay taxes on your Social Security benefits if your combined income* exceeds $25,000.

If you file a joint Federal tax return, you might have to pay taxes on your Social Security benefits if your combined income* exceeds 32,000.

If you are a member of a couple but file a separate Federal tax return, you probably will pay taxes on your Social Security benefits.

*"Combined income" means your adjusted gross income (as reported on your Form 1040) **plus** nontaxable interest **plus** one-half of your Social Security benefits.

As stated above, most people don't pay any taxes on their Social Security benefits. Of those few who do, nobody pays taxes on more than one-half of his or her benefits. Some pay taxes on a smaller amount of their benefits according to a formula developed by the Internal Revenue Service (IRS).

If you would like more information about the taxation of your Social Security benefits, there are some IRS publications that will help you. Call or visit IRS to ask for a copy of Publication 554, *Tax Benefits for Older Americans,* and Publication 915, *Tax Information on Social Security.*

When Somebody Needs Help Managing Benefits

Sometimes Social Security or SSI recipients are not able to handle their own financial affairs. In those cases, they turn to a relative, a friend, or another interested party to handle their Social Security matter. They call this person a "representative payee." All Social Security or SSI benefits due are made payable in the payee's name on behalf of the beneficiary.

If you are a representative payee, you have important responsibilities.

- You must use the Social Security or SSI benefits for the personal care and well-being of the beneficiary.

- You must keep Social Security informed of any events that might affect the beneficiary's eligibility for benefits. For example, you should tell them if the beneficiary moves or gets a job. And, of course, you should tell them when the beneficiary dies.
- You must file a periodic financial report with Social Security that shows how you spent the benefits you were paid.

If you would like to learn more about receiving benefits on behalf of another individual, call or visit any Social Security office to ask for a copy of the brochure, *A Guide For Representative Payees.*

Booklets Available

This book is intended to provide a general overview of Social Security programs and how they might affect you. Throughout this book there are references to other publications whenever the situation requires more information or a more detailed explanation.

The Social Security Administration and the Health Care Financing Administration (the Medicare people) produce many publications and fact sheets designed to help explain these programs. Here is a list of some you may find helpful.

- *Retirement*—A guide to Social Security retirement benefits.
- *Disability*—A guide to Social Security disability benefits.
- *Survivors*—A guide to Social Security survivors benefits.

- *Medicare*—A guide to the Medicare program.
- *Supplemental Security Income*—A guide to the SSI program.

These and other publications can be obtained free of charge at any Social Security office.

CHAPTER 5

Staying or Moving

CHAPTER 5

Staying or Moving

A place to live where you can be comfortable and happy, where you can have whatever care and services you need, is perhaps the most important single factor in determining whether your retirement years will be satisfying for you. Seventy-five percent of people retiring in America do not *move.* They stay were they have spent a good part of their lives. There are several factors that determine this. The children are born and raised in the house and have gone to school there. Other reasons include leaving a setting in which they are comfortable and have friends, relatives and sometimes children nearby, and a city they are familiar with. Sometimes it is close to where they have worked for many years and have established social relationships with former workers. Those are important reasons to consider for staying in their family home.

However it might be wise to evaluate the reasons and compare them with the economic facts of living in your present home. Here again you should take time and you should get advice from many people, people who have different kinds of wisdom to offer you: your family and friends, your banker, and your doctor. One major issue is: "Can I afford to stay in my house?" This question should be raised many years prior to retirement. It allows you to visit and explore other areas, other states. Advance inspection of many places can save serious mistakes. A vacation in the chosen places of retirement may indicate that it is unsuitable—or maybe, just the place you are looking for. It can also save you from unwise, sometimes unrecoverable investments in property or business. Searching for a place to retire to also helps your "retirement readiness." The more carefully retirement can be planned the greater the chance for success.

The following checklist is divided into 6 categories:

1. Social Requirements
2. Community
3. Work Opportunity
4. Health
5. Climate
6. General

Give the best possible answer to the question, and go over it several times to insure your feelings concerning certain questions.

1. SOCIAL REQUIREMENTS

WHAT DO I NEED TO FILL MY TIME			
	Important	Somewhat Important	Not Important
Social Clubs			
Sport Recreation			
Friends			
Family			
Theater			
Political Associations			
Restaurants			
Other			

1. COMMUNITY

WHAT TO EXPECT FROM A COMMUNITY			
	Important	Somewhat Important	Not Important
Affordable Housing			
Affordable Utilities			
Shopping Areas			
Low Crime Rate			
Public Transportation			
Restaurants			
Churches			
Theaters			
College			
Recreation			
Other			

1. WORK OPPORTUNITIES

OPPORTUNITY TO PROVIDE ADDITIONAL INCOME			
	Important	Somewhat Important	Not Important
Part-time Job Opportunity			
Full-time Job Opportunity			
Business, Manufacturing			
Business, Retail			
Business, Service			
Other			

1. HEALTH

HEALTH CARE SERVICES			
	Important	Somewhat Important	Not Important
Adequate Hospitals			
Doctors			
Dentists			
Medical Clinics			
Rest Homes			
Nursing Homes			
Mental Facilities			
Other			

1. CLIMATE

IS WEATHER IMPORTANT?			
	Important	Somewhat Important	Not Important
Weather			
Sunshine			
Rain			
Snow and Ice			
Humidity			
Hot Weather			
Moderate Weather			
Other			

1. GENERAL

WHAT ELSE IS IMPORTANT			
	Important	Somewhat Important	Not Important
Acceptable Traffic			
Family Nearby			
Friends Nearby			
Healthy Environment			
Good Water System			
Taxes			
Size of Town			
Getting Around			
Cost of Living			
Airport			
Other			

If you have answered all the questions let's review some of the results.

Under "Social Requirements," there are three choices: Important, Somewhat Important, and Not Important. The 7 questions deal with your social behavior. If you like to stay at home or you are the kind of person who has normally very little contact with other people, watch television and read books, your choice is easy. You do not need much outside activities and therefore can mark "Not Important" to most of the questions. But if you are a sports fan, watch outdoor games, hunt and fish with other couples and friends, you will certainly mark "Important" in several activities. This requirement will most likely continue in your next town or place. Because those activities are important to you and it will be a good part of your leisure time. This exercise will establish your social needs and requirements wherever you move to.

The second category is "Community." This is also a very important requirement to evaluate. It will determine if the place of your choice is acceptable in terms of affordability, public transportation, law and order, shopping, restaurants, etc. It is imperative to know what you like and what you need.

Most of the information in this category can be obtained from the Chamber of Commerce of any town of your choice. It is a good idea to request the information about the town or the area from the Chamber of Commerce prior to your visit. It allows you to review the material at your leisure. The package you receive includes the real estate market value, utility cost, the climate and other information you need to make a sensible decision.

Take your time answering the questions and give
it serious consideration.

The third category deals with "Work Opportunity." A significant matter—if you desire to work
during retirement, part-time or full-time. It is of
considerable importance to know what opportunities
exist in your new community. Especially if you are
thinking of starting a new business. Let's assume that
you are considering a "craft store" in your newly
found town, you would like to know how many
other similar stores you have to compete with. You
may like to work part-time or full-time for a firm or
an office. Find out what the possibilities are. Prepare
before you move.

The fourth category is about "Health." It is
essential that good health care is available. The seven
questions give you an idea of what to look for. Make
sure that there are good doctors in town or in the
area. General practitioners, and specialists. Establish
doctors who accept medicare and your insurance. Do
the same for hospitals, clinics, etc. The Chamber of
Commerce will most likely include a list of doctors
and hospitals. A good idea is to order a telephone
book, especially the yellow pages, of your new home
town. The yellow pages have a wealth of information
and provide you with what's available.

If you are interested in retirement homes, make
sure to visit them! You might not have a requirement for it at the present time but it is good to know
what quality homes are available, and how much
they cost.

The next category is "Climate." Weather can be
very important. Dealing with severe snow, humidity
or hot weather can be a strain on your condition and
personality. The Chamber of Commerce can provide

you with weather information. They provide the temperature range from January through December, the snowfall (if any) and rainfall in inches per month or per year. Visit the town or area several times during the year to experience the local weather.

The last category is a general one. It deals with a variety of issues that you may consider or require. The size of a town can be important. The traffic, will be most likely lighter, in a smaller or medium-sized city. It will be easier getting around. Other considerations are healthy environment, air quality, good water system and supply. You may also require an airport nearby for your travel and good access to your friends and family.

Final Word About Moving

If you plan to move, the questions you have answered are part of your preparations. It will help you to be ready for retirement. You do not have to feel old to deal with retirement. You stay younger and healthier if you plan wisely.

If you plan to buy or rent a home, maintenance will be part of your daily or weekly duties. Inside requires cleaning, bed making, dusting, scrubbing, and household repairs. Outside requires snow shoveling, leaf raking, painting, roof repairing, etc. When choosing a house you should consider the location of your home, upstairs, downstairs, uphill, downhill. You might be able to run upstairs today with no trouble but at 80 it might restrict you from leaving the house more than once a day. If the house is level with the street it reduces the strain and you can enjoy the outdoors more often.

The house you retire to should not wear you out before your time. Be sure that the home you plan to retire in can be kept up with minimum work and risk. Not only for your health, but it also reduces expenditures. Repair bills, as well as medical and general bills, can be kept to a minimum by proper planning.

CHAPTER 6

Retirement and the Law

- Retiring Safely
- Protect Yourself

CHAPTER 6

Retiring Safely

You may wonder why a chapter on Retirement and the Law. The reason is, that when you retire, your margin for error begins to disappear, so it is important to avoid mistakes if you can. As a young working man or woman, you could recoup your losses if you made a mistake. Now you may not have a chance to do so.

And never before in our history have older Americans had such a wide variety of decisions to make. You, and all the other Americans over 65, have a combined annual income of some $35 billion. *So you are now a market.* People who sell housing and goods and services of all kinds want to sell to you. Most of these businessmen are reputable, but many are not. So you need to choose wisely from all that is offered you to buy—and you need to choose wisely the businessmen with whom you deal. Make your decisions carefully.

And make your decisions early. The sooner you start on your plans for retirement, the better. You are more likely to make them wisely if you tackle them well in advance, while you have time for full consideration. Many preparations for the adjustments of retirement must be made while you are still working.

Let's identify areas of concern, matters that are important as you near your retirement age.

- Buying or selling your home.
- Starting a business as an individual or partnership.

- Signing contracts of any kind.
- Establishing or revising a will.
- Establishing a trust fund.
- Borrowing funds from institutions.
- Loaning money to anybody.
- Investing
- Donating substantial assets.

Not all matters can be listed here; we have only identified a few. It should be emphasized that in all probability you will go through your retirement without having to call a lawyer except for a few matters. But the retirement years have many legal problems and a lawyer is good to have.

The Family Lawyer

You will do well to choose "a family lawyer" if you do not already have one. He can give you a legal checkup.

You are used to having a physical checkup from time to time to find out how you are. Then, the doctor lets you know if there are any problems developing which need attention. In the same way, a lawyer can go over your legal situation with you. He can then determine whether there areany steps you should take to protect yourself or your family—such as making or revising a will. And in the process, you and the lawyer will get to know each other and he will then be available as new problems come up or new decisions need to be made.

You can arrange for periodic consultations also, since laws and circumstances change as the years go by. You should by all means have a new legal checkup whenever there is any major change in your circumstances—such as a death in the family, or a birth, a marriage, divorce, or a change in your financial condition whether for better or worse.

And it is of the utmost importance to have a new checkup if you move from one state to another. The laws of each state are different in many important respects. For example, the laws of inheritance differ from state to state. A valid will in one state may not be valid in another. Remember it is the law of the state where you make your home which determines the validity of your will. There are other important legal matters which may be affected if you move across state lines.

The law is designed to help people. So use the law to help you—don't let it trip you up.

How To Look For A Lawyer

It may take some time and effort to locate the lawyer who will be right for you. Fortunately, when you are looking for a family lawyer to advise you about things before they happen, you can take your time. This is quite different from the mad dash a person must make to find someone to represent him when he is in a jam. And the time spent in selecting your lawyer carefully is well invested. It will increase your satisfaction with the service you get.

The best way to select a lawyer is to find a *satisfied* client. Talk to your family and friends. See if any of them have used the services of a lawyer and if they were satisfied. You should ask, also, what sort of matters the lawyer handled for them. Some lawyers, particularly in large cities, specialize in certain branches of the law and are not interested in handling matters outside their specialty. They are not family lawyers.

There may be a lawyer referral service where you live or at the county seat. Such a service is sponsored and supervised by the local bar association. If there is one, you will find it listed in the telephone book. The referral service can give you the name of a reliable attorney and you can have a first interview with him for a stated—and very modest—fee. In that interview, you can find out whether you will need further legal services and, if so, you can decide whether you want to continue with the lawyer to whom you were referred. You will be under no obligation to do so if you do not want to.

Many city and state offices on aging and many local senior centers have "lay advocates" or "paralegals," who have not been through law school but who do have legal training, to give advice and other assistance to seniors. Their services are either free or low-cost. Also see if your community has a legal clinic, which probably has a staff of several lawyers and can offer legal advice on a high-volume, low-cost basis. Some university law schools have established free legal clinics.

How A Lawyer Serves You

The lawyer's primary responsibility, of course, is to advise you about the legal aspects of your affairs and, if indicated, to use legal procedures for handling them. He may draw up a will, a deed, or a contract, or look over documents of this sort that have been prepared by someone else such as a real estate agent to see that your interests are protected adequately. He/she may negotiate with others on your behalf.

A lawyer will not necessarily go to court for you. He will do that only if you are being sued or if you have a legal claim which cannot be settled satisfactorily by negotiation. Because of his general knowledge of people and business, he may advise you about various aspects of your affairs which are not entirely matters of law, or he may call on experts from other fields, or suggest that you doso.

You will want to know, of course, how much the lawyer will charge you for his work. And rightly so. It is businesslike to know what you will have to pay for what you get. Always ask in advance.

Ordinarily a lawyer charges on the basis of the amount of time he spends in serving you. This includes the time spent in talking to you in his office and on the telephone, looking up the law, preparing legal documents, writing letters, etc. You can help yourself in this regard by discussing your affairs clearly and concisely. It is also advisable to limit your contacts with the lawyer to the appointments which he suggests, unless there are developments of real importance which he should know.

Attorneys sometimes set a flat fee for certain types of work, such as drawing a will, probating a decedent's estate, or handling a real estate transaction. In some cases they charge a percentage of the amount collected by the client or awarded to him by a court. In such cases, the attorney gets no fee at all if the case is lost. Although some lawyers get very substantial fees in difficult cases or ones involving large sums of money, their fees are generally reasonable for the services they perform.

In your first consultation with a lawyer, or in consulting him about a new matter, you should ask him the basis on which he will set his fee. If it is on an hourlybasis, find out what his rate per hour is. The attorney may be able to give you a rough estimate of the total cost even though he does charge on an hourly basis.

For certain kinds of legal work, a lawyer's fee is subject to approval by a court or by a State or Federal agency. For example, the lawyer's fee is controlled in cases involving guardianships and estates of deceased persons and in proceedings concerning certain types of retirement benefits such as social security.

Fees are sometimes adjusted on the basis of the client's ability to pay. If the attorney asks you for a financial statement, give it to him fully and accurately. Such a statement may result in a lower fee rather than a higher one.

Sometimes clients wonder why it is necessary to pay any fee if the lawyer does not go to court or prepare some legal document. But giving advice *before* something happens also can be time consuming and is often the most valuable service a lawyer can give to his clients. Seeing a lawyer before difficulties arise is often better—and less expensive in the long run—than seeing one after difficulties are upon you.

When To See A Lawyer About Someone To Look After Things For You

Whatever your living arrangements, you should plan for someone to look after things for you if you should become very ill—and for someone to know if you do. If you plan ahead, it is more likely that things will be taken care of the way you want. In an emergency, you might not feel up to making plans for yourself. Others might hesitate to make them for you.

There are different ways you can give another person legal authority to look after things for you. The best way for you will depend upon your circumstances. Your lawyer can help you decide which to choose. He can prepare, or review, papers for you to sign to confer legal authority on the agent of your choice.

Placing some or all of your assets in joint ownership or under joint control is one way to provide for someone else to act for you. Joint ownership or control can be tricky. The legal implications depend upon the exact wording of the ownership clause or control agreement and on the laws of the several States. The question of the true ownership of your assets is also raised: do they still belong to you alone or does the arrangement constitute a gift by you to the other person, at least as far as any balance is concerned. And once joint ownership is established, the other person can act alone at any time whether you are ill or not. So do not place your assets in joint ownership or under joint control *before* you have talked to your lawyer.

Power Of Attorney

A power of attorney is a document which you sign giving another person power to act for you as your attorney. (In this case the word "attorney" means agent, not lawyer.) It can be limited to certain acts or it can authorize the other person to act for you in all matters. Like joint ownership or control, the other person has the right to act at any time whether you are sick or well.

If you use this method, have your lawyer prepare the power of attorney. Do not buy a printed form and fill it in yourself. Doing it properly is a protection to you, to the person who acts for you, and to those with whom he deals.

Going Into Business For Yourself

Some people go into business for themselves after they retire. This is "earning extra money" on a more formal basis. Some retirees run a small grocery store, make furniture, run a gift shop, or manage real estate. You can get valuable advice on how to start and manage a business from the Small Business Administration. There may be a branch office of the SBA, listed in your local phone book.

If you do go into business for yourself, you should, by all means, talk over your plans with a lawyer before you start. You should also use him as a consultant while you are carrying on your business. And, if you should close out your enterprise, have the family lawyer supervise your procedures. Advice from your lawyer can help you take advantage of favorable legal provisions and it can also help you avoid taking any action unwittingly which might expose you to civil—or even criminal—liability. Proper procedures in closing out a business, for example, define the extent of your rights and liabilities in relation to others.

The way in which your business is structured—as an individual enterprise, a partnership, or a corporation—may spell the difference between success and failure. Partnerships, by the way, can be tricky. Never—but never—enter into one without first getting advice from a lawyer.

Trusts

A trust involves transferring the legal title to some or all of your assets to another person for a specified use for your benefit. For your protection, an arrangement of this sort should be based on a trust agreement prepared by your lawyer and signed by you and the other person. It should set forth the manner in which you want your property used for your benefit and the disposition to be made of any remaining balance at the time of your death.

Trusts are often used by people of substantial wealth, usually with a bank or trust company acting as trustee. Trusts can also be used by people of moderate means if they can find someone who is willing to act as trustee for them, either free of charge or for a modest fee.

Should You Make A Will

You are probably wondering if you should make a will. You *should* by all means make one if you are in business or if you have promised to leave your estate in return for care and support. Whether or not you should make a will in any event, is one of the things you ought to discuss with your lawyer.

If you do make a will, or revise one you have already made, have your lawyer prepare it. Do not buy a legal form and fill it in yourself. When used in a will, words can have a meaning that is quite different from their meaning in common usage. If you don't have enough to leave to make it worth your while to pay a lawyer to draw your will, the chances are that you don't have enough to leave to warrant making a will at all.

Also have your lawyer supervise the way in which you and your witnesses sign the will. There are formal requirements for the way in which this is done. If they are not carried out, your will won't be valid. And a will which is not valid is no will at all.

If you move to another State, find out if you need to make a new will. The laws relating to wills may be different in the new State or the witnesses to your old will might not be readily available to prove up your will in the area of your new residence.

Even if you do not move, your will should be reviewed from time to time, especially after a change in financial or family circumstances.

Joint Tenancy

Joint tenancy is sometimes called "The Poor Man's Will." Land or other property, such as bank accounts, stocks, bonds, cars, etc., can be owned by several persons during their lifetime, with the provision that a surviving owner retain rights to all the property remaining upon the deaths of the other owners.

This device can be, and often is, used to provide for the disposition of property after death. The effect of joint ownership depends upon the wording of the ownership clause and the applicable State law. A will, even if you have made one, would have no effect upon assets owned in this manner. Since joint tenancy can be tricky, be sure to get legal advice if you want to use this means of disposing of your property. You and your joint tenant may want to make wills affecting the property remaining at the death of the survivor. In fact it may be advisable to do so while you can talk over what ultimate disposition is to be made. When the time comes that either you or your joint tenant dies, it could be that the survivor might then be too ill—or forgetful—to make a will.

Naming A Beneficiary

With certain kinds of benefits such as life insurance, you can name a beneficiary to receive the benefits after your death. This may also be true for pension benefits or annuities. This is something to ask about if you are in a private pension plan or have an annuity.

Finally....

Whether or not you work to earn money when you retire, you will want to be as busy and active as you can. You will want to get out and mix with other people, learn something new, or learn more about something you already know. This is good. Much of what you do will have little or no connection with the law. But some activities can involve you in legal transactions—they can involve you in contracts to pay substantial sums of money either in advance or on the installment plan.

Before you sign a contract for membership in a club, or for a course of instruction, or to buy equipment to use in pursuing your activity—stop, look, and listen. Find out all you can about whatever it is you are paying for—or promising to pay for. Find out all you can about the people with whom you are dealing. Ask for advice and listen to it.

Remember, you can't buy love. Don't let your longing for affection, or companionship, or activity trap you into spending your money foolishly.

Good planning, with a good legal structure to support it, can go far toward making you comfortable and happy and secure in the years ahead.

Protect Yourself

As we mentioned earlier in this book the retired population of America is a significant group. Companies cater specifically to that market. Most companies are legitimate and have an excellent reputation. But, be careful and choose wisely. Make sure you are dealing with reputable companies. Check their local Chamber of Commerce or Better Business Bureau and ask for references.

One of the areas you must be cautioned about is telemarketing and high pressure sales people. Telephone sales is a growing industry and, again, most of them arelegitimate. Here are some tips to watch for telemarketing fraud.

1. Eight Facts You Should Know About Telemarketing

1. **Most—but not all—telephone sales calls are made by legitimate businesses offering legitimate products or services.** But wherever honest firms search for new customers, so do swindlers. Phone fraud is a multi-billion dollar business that involves selling everything from bad or non-existent investments to the peddling of misrepresented products and services! Everyone who has a phone is a prospect; whether you become a victim is largely up to you.

2. There is no way to positively determine whether a sales call is on the up and up simply by talking with someone on the phone. No matter what questions you ask or how many you ask, skilled swindlers have ready answers. That's why sales calls from persons or organizations that are unknown to you should always be checked out before you actually buy or invest. Legitimate callers have nothing to hide.

3. Phone swindlers are likely to know more about *you* than you know about *them*. Depending on where they got your name in the first place, they may know your age and income, health and hobbies, occupation and marital status, education, the home you live in, what magazines you read and whether you've bought by phone in the past.

Even if your name came from the phone book, telephone con men (and women) assume that, like most people, you would be interested in having more income, that you're receptive to a bargain, that you are basically sympathetic to people in need, and that you are reluctant to be discourteous to someone on the phone. As admirable as such characteristics may be, they help make the swindler's job easier. Swindlers also exploit less admirable characteristics, such as greed.

4. Fraudulent sales callers have one thing in common: They are skilled liars and experts at verbal camouflage. Their success depends on it. Many are coached to "say whatever it takes" by operators of the "boiler rooms" where they work at rows of phone desks making hundreds of repetitious calls, hour after hour. The first words uttered by most victims of phone fraud are, "the caller sounded so believable...."

5. Perpetrators of phone fraud are extremely good at sounding as though they represent legitimate businesses. They offer investments, sell subscriptions, provide products for homes and offices, promote travel and vacation plans, describe employment opportunities, solicit donations, and the list goes on. Never assume you'll "know a phone scam when you hear one." Even if you've read lists of the kinds of schemes most commonly practiced, innovative swindlers constantly devise new ones.

6. The motto of phone swindlers is, "just give us a few good 'mooches,'" one of the terms they use to describe their victims. Notwithstanding that most victims are otherwise intelligent and prudent people, even boiler room operators express astonishment at how many people "seem to keep their checkbooks by the telephone!" Sadly, some families part with savings they worked years to accumulate on the basis of little more than a 15-minute phone conversation—less time than they spend considering the purchase of a household appliance!

7. The person who "initiates" the phone call may be *you*. It's not uncommon for phone crooks to use direct mailings and advertise in reputable publications to encourage prospects to make the initial contact. It's another way swindlers imitate the perfectly acceptable marketing practices of legitimate businesses. Although you may have written or phoned for "additional information" about an investment, product, or service, you should remain cautious about buying, by phone, from someone you don't know.

8. Victims of phone fraud seldom get their money back—or, at best, no more than a few cents on the dollar. Despite efforts of law enforcement and regulatory agencies to provide what help they can to victims, swindlers generally do the same thing other people do when they get money: they *spend* it!

2. Nine Tip-Offs That The Caller Could Be A Crook

1. High-pressure sales tactics. The call may not begin that way, but if the swindler senses you're not going to be an easy sale, he or she may shift to a hard sell. This is in contrast to legitimate businesses, most of which respect an individual's right to be "not interested."

High-pressure sales tactics take a variety of forms but the common denominator is usually a stubborn reluctance to accept "no" as an answer. Some callers may resort to insult and argument, questioning the prospect's intelligence or ability to make a decision, often ending with a warning that "you're going to be very sorry if you don't do such and such." Or, "you'll never get rich if you don't take a chance."

2. Insistence on an immediate decision. If it's an investment, the caller may say something like, "the market is starting to move even as we talk." For a product or service, the urgency pitch may be that "there are only a few left" or "the offer is about to expire." The bottom line is that swindlers often insist that you should (or must) make your decision *right now*. And they always give a reason.

3. The offer sounds too good to be true. The oldest advice around is still the best: "An offer that sounds too good to be true probably is." Having said this, however, you should be aware that some phone swindlers are becoming more sophisticated. They may make statements that sound just reasonable enough (if only barely) to keep you from hanging up. Or they may make three or four statements you know to be true so that when they spring the big lie for what they're selling, you'll be more likely to believe that, too. That's where the verbal camouflage comes in.

4. A request for your credit card number for any purpose other than to make a purchase. A swindler may ask you for your credit card number— or, in the most brash cases, several credit card num-bers—for "identification," or "verification" that you have won something, or merely as an "expression of good faith" on your part. Whatever the ploy, once a swindler has your card number it is likely that unau-thorized charges will appear on your account!

5. An offer to send someone to your home or office to pick up the money, or some other method such as overnight mail to get your funds more quickly. This is likely to be part of their "ur-gency" pitch. It could be an effort to avoid mail fraud charges by bypassing postal authorities or simply a way of getting your money before you change your mind.

6. A statement that something is "free," followed by a requirement that you pay for something. While honest firms may promote free phone offers to attract customers, the difference with swindlers is that you generally have to *pay* in some way to get whatever it is that's "free." The cost may be labeled as a handling or shipping charge, or as payment for an item in addition to the "prize." Whatever you receive "free"—if anything—most likely will be worth much less than what you've paid.

7. An investment that's "without risk." Except for obligations of the U.S. Government, *all* investments have some degree of risk. And if there were any such thing as a risk-free investment with big profits assured, the caller certainly wouldn't have to dial through the phone book to find investors!

8. Unwillingness to provide written information or references (such as a bank or names of satisfied customers in your area) that you can contact. Swindlers generally have a long list of reasons: "There isn't time for that," or "it's a brand new offer and printed material isn't available yet," or "customer references would violate someone's privacy." Even with references, be cautious, some swindlers pay off a few customers—to serve as unwitting references.

The caller may also be reluctant to answer *questions* by phone—such as inquiries about the firm or even how and where you can contact the firm. The swindler may insist on contacting you later "for your convenience."

9. A suggestion that you should make a purchase or investment on the basis of "trust." Trust is a laudable trait, but it shouldn't be dispensed indiscriminately —certainly not to unknown persons calling on the phone and asking that you send them money. Even so, "trust me" is a pitch that swindlers sometimes employ when all else fails.

3. Ten Ways To Avoid Becoming A Victim

1. Don't allow yourself to be pushed into a hurried decision. No matter what you're told to the contrary, the reality is that at least 99 percent of everything that's a good deal today will still be a good deal a week from now! And the other one percent isn't generally worth the risk you'd be taking to find out.

There may be times when you'll want to make a prompt decision, but those occasions shouldn't involve an irrevocable financial commitment to purchase a product or make an investment that you're not familiar with from a caller that you don't know. And purchase decisions should never be made under pressure.

2. Always request written information, by mail, about the product, service, investment or charity and about the organization that's offering it. For legitimate firms, this shouldn't be a problem. Swindlers, however, may not want to give you time for adequate consideration, may not have written material available, or may not want to risk a run-in with legal or regulatory authorities by putting fraudulent statements in writing.

Also insist on having enough time to study any information provided before being contacted again or agreeing to meet with anyone in person. Some high-pressure telephone sales calls are solely for the purpose of persuading you to meet with an even higher-pressure sales person in your home!

3. Don't make any investment or purchase you don't fully understand. The beauty of the American economy is the diversity of investment vehicles and other products available. But it's a diversity that includes the bad as well as the good. Unless you fully understand what you'd be buying or investing, you can be *badly* burned. Swindlers intentionally seek out individuals who *don't* know what they are doing! They often attempt to flatter prospects into *thinking* they are making an informed decision.

4. Ask what state or federal agencies the firm is regulated by and/or is required to be registered with. And if you get an answer, ask for a phone number or address that you can use to contact the agency and verify the answer yourself. If the firm says it's not subject to any regulation, you may want to increase your level of caution swiftly.

5. Check out the company or organization. Don't assume a firm wouldn't provide you with information, references, or regulatory contacts unless the information was accurate and reliable. That's precisely what swindlers *want* you to assume! They know that most people never bother to follow through. Look at it this way: most victims of fraud contact a regulatory agency *after* they've lost their money; it's far better to make the contact and obtain whatever information is available while you still *have* your money!

6. **If an investment or major purchase is involved, request that information also be sent to your accountant, financial advisor, banker, or attorney for evaluation and an opinion.** Swindlers don't want you to seek a second opinion. Their reluctance or evasiveness could be your tip-off.

7. **Ask what recourse you would have if you make a purchase and aren't satisfied.** If there's a guarantee or refund provision, it's best to have it in writing and be satisfied that the business will stand behind its guarantee before you make a final financial commitment.

8. **Beware of testimonials that you may have no way of checking out.** They may involve nothing more than someone being paid a fee to speak well of a product or service.

9. **Don't provide any personal financial information over the phone unless you are absolutely certain the caller has a real need to know.** That goes especially for your credit card numbers and bank account information. The *only* time you should give anyone your credit card number is if you've decided to make a purchase and want to charge it. If someone says they'll send a bill later but they need your credit card number in the meantime, be cautious and be certain you're dealing with a reputable company.

10. If necessary, hang up. If you're simply not interested, if you become subject to high-pressure sales tactics, if you can't obtain the information you want or get evasive answers, or if you hear your own better judgment whispering that you may be making a serious mistake, just say good-bye.

CHAPTER 7

Stay Active and Healthy

CHAPTER 7

Stay Active and Healthy

Older people are now living longer than any generation in history. This is no accident. People take better care of themselves, read more labels on food packages and promote better fitness. Medical science is making it possible to extend life and maintain health and energy.

A proper diet and exercise can reduce susceptibility to illness and increase longevity. One physician, commenting on aging, said: "Most of us don't wear out, we rust out." Disuse is the mortal enemy of the human body.

Growing older must not mean inactivity or infirmity. Experts tell us that fitness can be defined in two main categories:

1. Organic Fitness

Good organic health, that is, a well-nourished body free of disease or infirmity. Maintaining a healthy diet of body building food.

2. Dynamic Fitness

Though free of disease, the body may still not be fully fit. Dynamic fitness promotes the efficiency of the heart and lungs, muscular strength and endurance, balance, flexibility and coordination.

Both, organic and dynamic fitness, require professional advice and a step-by-step program by established health organizations. Before you make an attempt to make changes in your life in terms of diet or start exercising, see your doctor for a clean bill of health. A complete physical and discussing your plans with your doctor is a good start. Many studies conducted on longevity show exercise promotes a healthy body and slows down the aging process. The circulation of your blood supply and the oxygen, during exercise, keep your organs in excellent shape and your body agile. Other benefits associated with a good exercise program can be:

- Lower blood pressure
- Reduces weight
- Good blood circulation
- Increases endurance
- Reduces stress
- More restful
- Better appearance
- More active

and can help reduce:

- Heart problems
- Arthritis
- Headaches
- Indigestion

A well-supervised exercise program can keep you drug free and will help extend your retirement years with good health. Exercise also stimulates an active interest in living mentally and physically. Make your organic fitness and your dynamic fitness a top priority in your retirement years.

Maintain a keen awareness of healthy facts and age-related changes. It helps preserve good health and fitness. By learning about normal changes that occur when people get older, and techniques of preventive care, older people can take an active roll in maintaining a healthy, independent life style for as long as possible.

The following facts offer practical advice on health promotion to older people. These facts are supported by National Institute of Health and Department of Health and Human Services.

1. Finding Good Medical Care
2. What To Do About The Flu
3. Don't Take It Easy
4. Nutrition
5. Safe Use Of Medicines
6. Accidents And The Elderly
7. Can Life Be Extended?
8. Health Quackery

1. FINDING GOOD MEDICAL CARE

Finding the best possible medical care, a difficult search at any time of life, becomes more difficult just as you begin to need it most—after reaching age 60 or 70.

While most older people are basically healthy and report themselves in good to excellent health, many tend to underreport specific health problems and mistakenly think they are caused by "old age" rather than disease. Yet old age does affect people's health, mainly by causing them to react differently to various diseases and drugs. For example:

- Some diseases may show different signs in older people. For example, a heart attack may occur in an older person without chest pains and appendicitis may occur without the same abdominal tenderness that a younger person usually experiences.

- An older person may have several health problems and take several medications at the same time. These often interact and cause a confusing array of symptoms and reactions that need to be considered in deciding upon the proper medical treatment.
- Drugs act differently in older people than in the young, making unusual reactions from drugs more likely with increasing age.

The older person needs a doctor who is aware of these special needs and problems. But finding such a person may be difficult because doctors in the United States do not routinely receive special training in the care of the elderly, relying mainly upon personal experience. Only recently has geriatrics—the study of the care of the aged—begun to be included in medical school curriculum. Geriatrics is not a separate medical specialty like pediatrics or cardiology.

Another problem is that many older people who have been treated by the same doctor over the years lose their family doctor to retirement or death.

The health care of the aged should improve, however. The over-65 age group is expected to constitute 20 percent of the population by the year 2030 (versus 11 percent today and 4 percent in 1900). As the number of older persons increases, so should the number of medical students and practicing physicians studying geriatrics.

As a start toward finding a doctor who has a special interest in treating older people, you can contact your county medical society or state agency on aging. Other possible sources of information include local referral services, medical schools, or university medical centers.

The following checklist may help you in finding a new doctor or dentist or in evaluating your present one:

- Are you comfortable with your doctor? Can you openly discuss your feelings and talk about personal concerns such as sexual and emotional problems?
- Do you believe your doctor will stand by you, no matter how difficult your problems be come?
- Does your doctor listen to you and answer all your questions about the causes and treatment of your physical problems? Or is he or she vague, impatient, or unwilling to answer?
- Does your doctor take a thorough "medical history" on you and ask about past physical and emotional problems, family medical history, drugs you are taking, and other matters affecting your health?
- Does your doctor seem to automatically prescribe drugs rather than deal with the real causes of your medical problems?
- Does your doctor attribute your problems to "old age"?
- Does your doctor have an associate to whom you can turn should your doctor retire or die?

Unfortunately, some doctors still equate aging with inevitable mental and physical decline. Dr. Robert N. Butler, former Director of the National Institute on Aging, tells of a 101-year-old man who complained to his doctor about a pain in his left leg.

"Well," said the doctor, "what can you expect at your age?" The man replied, "But doctor, my right leg also is 101, and it doesn't hurt a bit!"

Remember that, like the man in the story, you are a consumer, entitled to ask questions when selecting a doctor and to expect reasonable, satisfying answers, not age-worn cliches.

A good doctor-patient relationship is based upon mutual respect and open communication. The doctor should allow you an active role in deciding when to seek medical attention, whether to accept the doctor's advice, and when to seek asecond opinion from another doctor. And you, the patient, owe your physician cooperation and honesty, and owe yourself a continuing interest in seeking the best medical care.

2. WHAT TO DO ABOUT FLU

Each winter, millions of people suffer from the unpleasant effects of the "flu." For most of these people, a few days in bed, a few more days of rest, aspirin, and plenty to drink will be the best treatment.

Flu—the short name for influenza—is usually a mild disease in healthy children, young adults, and middle-aged people. But, in older people or in those of any age who have chronic illnesses, flu can be life-threatening. By lowering a person's resistance, flu may allow more serious infections to occur, especially pneumonia.

It is easy to confuse a common cold with influenza. An important difference is that flu causes fever, usually absent during a cold. Also, nasal congestion occurs more often with a cold than with the flu. Cold symptoms generally are milder and don't last as long as symptoms of the flu.

Flu is a viral infection of the nose, throat, and lungs. It spreads quickly from one person to another, particularly in crowded places such as buses, theaters, hospitals, and schools.

Because of its ability to spread rapidly, flu was once believed to be caused by the influence of the stars and planets. In the 1500's the Italians gave the disease the name "influenza," their word for "influence."

What Causes Flu?

Not until the 1930's and 1940's did scientists discover that flu is caused by constantly changing types of viruses. These tiny parasites invade animals and human beings and begin to multiply rapidly. Disease appears when their number grows too large for the body's immune system to fight off immediately.

When someone infected with the flu coughs or sneezes, droplets containing the virus particles may reach another person, entering the body through the respiratory system. There, the viruses can multiply and cause the flu.

Symptoms

The effects of a flu infection can differ from person to person. Sometimes flu will cause no obvious symptoms. Often, however, the patient will feel weak and will develop a cough, a headache, and a sudden rise in temperature. The fever can last anywhere from 1 to 6 days. Other symptoms include aching muscles; chills; and red, watery eyes.

Complications of Flu

Flu is rarely a fatal illness. But while the immune system is busy fighting off the flu, a person is less able to resist a second infection. If this second infection is in the lungs, it could be life-threatening. Older people and people with chronic diseases (such as heart disease, emphysema, asthma, bronchitis, kidney disease, and diabetes) are at the greatest risk of developing secondary infections. The most serious of these is pneumonia, one of the five leading causes of death among people over 65.

Pneumonia—an inflammation of the lungs— may be caused by a flu virus. More often, however, it results from bacteria that multiplied in the system during a flu infection.

The symptoms of pneumonia are somewhat similar to those of the flu but are much more severe. Shaking chills are very common, and coughing becomes more frequent and may produce a colored discharge. The fever that accompanies the flu will continue during pneumonia and will stay high. Pain in the chest may occur as the lungs become more inflamed.

Bacterial pneumonia is usually treated with penicillin. This antibiotic drug, which kills the bacteria, is very effective if given early enough in the course of the disease. During the most serious phase of pneumonia, the body loses essential fluids. Patients therefore often receive extra fluids to prevent shock, a dangerous conditionmarked by inadequate blood flow.

Prevention

Because the elderly are prone to develop pneumonia along with the flu, many doctors recommend that their older patients get a flu shot (or vaccination) in the early fall. Side effects will sometimes occur, such as a low fever or a redness at the injection site. But in most people the dangers from getting flu and possibly pneumonia are considered greater than the dangers from the side effects of the flu shot. One exception is people who have allergies to eggs: flu vaccines are made using egg products and may cause reactions in those with such allergies.

Preventing flu is difficult because flu viruses change constantly and unpredictably. This year's virus usually is slightly different from last year's. The difference generally is just enough to get by the defenses produced by the last flu shot. Therefore, flu shots are effective for only 1 year.

Treatment

Vaccination remains the most commonly used method of preventing influenza. In recent years, the use of an antiviral drug, amantadine, has also been recommended for the prevention and treatment of many types of influenza, particularly in high-risk individuals. However, the usual recommended treatment is: (1) take aspirin for the aches and pains, (2) drink plenty of fluids, and (3) stay in bed until the fever has been gone for 1 or 2 days. It is especially important to stay rested, since the fever may return if the patient becomes too active too soon. If the fever persists, a doctor should be called, since this may mean that a more serious infection is present.

Scientists continue to look for ways to prevent and treat influenza. In the meantime, the Public Health Service's Advisory Committee on Immunization Practices encourages those over 65 and others with chronic illnesses to get an annual vaccination.

3. DON'T TAKE IT EASY—EXERCISE!

If exercise could be packed into a pill, it would be the single most widely prescribed, and beneficial, medicine in the Nation, said Robert N. Butler, M.D., former Director, National Institute on Aging. Each year, more scientific evidence points to the truth of this statement. Regular physical activity can help the human body maintain, repair, and improve itself to an amazing degree. And most older people—even those with illnesses or disabilities—can take part in moderate exercise programs.

Anyone planning to start a fitness program should see a doctor first. Those with medical problems may have to avoid some kinds of exercise or adjust their levels of activity. But even people who are confined to wheelchairs can do many exercises to improve their strength and sense of well-being.

Many older people enjoy exercises such as walking, swimming, and bicycle riding. But there are other possibilities, such as modified aerobic dancing, calisthenics, and yoga. People who have kept in good condition may be able to participate in a wider range of activities.

It is very important to tailor your program to fit your own level of ability and special needs. For example, jogging is not for everyone and may be dangerous for those who have unsuspected heart disease.

The Benefits of Exercise

Exercise will strengthen your heart and lungs, lower your blood pressure, and protect against the start of adult-onset diabetes. Exercise can even strengthen your bones, slowing down the progress of osteoporosis, a bone-thinning disorder in women. It also strengthens and tones your muscles and helps you move about more easily by keeping joints, tendons, and ligaments more flexible.

When combined with good eating habits, exercise can help you lose weight by burning excess fat tissue and helpingcontrol your appetite. Exercise may also give you more energy, help you sleep better and feel less tense, improve your appearance and self-confidence, and contribute to good mental health by keeping you socially and sexually active.

Designing an Exercise Program

Anyone who has been inactive for many years should never try to do too much too soon. Start by seeing a doctor, especially if you are over 50, if you have a disease or disability, or you are taking any medication regularly. Your doctor can evaluate your physical condition, help you decide which activity will suit you best, and check your progress after the exercise program is under way.

It is important to choose an activity you enjoy. Decide whether you want to join a group, exercise with a friend, or exercise alone. If you exercise alone, tell someone of your schedule and plans in case you need assistance. See if you prefer an outdoor or indoor activity, and decide what time of day is best for you. You may have to try different activities and times before you make your exercise period a routine part of your schedule.

Begin by exercising slowly, especially if you have been inactive. Start with short periods of about 5 to 10 minutes twice a week. Then build up slowly—adding no more than a few minutes each week. If all goes well, as it probablywill, slowly increase your exercise periods to 15 to 30 minutes, 3 or 4 times a week. Your doctor may advise stretching as well as warm-up and cool-down periods of 5 to 15 minutes to tune up your body before exercise and to help you wind down afterwards. You can simply stretch and then do the same activity, or a similar one, at a slower pace.

Always pay attention to what your body tells you. If you feel much discomfort, you are trying to do too much. Ease up a bit, or take a break and start again at another time. Although most people will have no problems if they start exercising slowly, be alert to unusual symptoms such as chest pain, breathlessness, joint discomfort, or muscle cramps. Call your doctor if any of these occurs.

Finding an Exercise Program

Many communities have centers where older people can join exercise classes and other recreational programs. Find out about fitness programs at a local church or synagogue, civic center, community college, park or recreation association, senior citizens' center, or service organization (such as an area agency on aging). Area Jewish Community Center, YMCAs, and YWCAs usually offer a variety of programs. Organized activities designed for older adults provide many benefits to people who have been inactive or to those with health problems.

If you work, ask about programs there. Knowing that fitness improves performance on the job, many companies provide opportunities for their employees to exercise regularly.

If you are convinced that regular exercise is not for you, try to stay active in other ways. Activities such as bowling, square dancing, fishing, nature walks, arts and crafts, card and table games, gardening, and community projects will not offer all the benefits of regular, moderate exercise. But they will help you remain actively involved in life, possibly adding years to your own.

4. NUTRITION

The basic guidelines for a nutritious diet are the same for most healthy adults. Older people, however, need to pay special attention to the quality of the foods they eat.

Most people gain weight more easily as they age. Because of changes in the body and decreasing physical activity, older people usually need fewer calories. The requirement for nutrients such as proteins, carbohydrates, vitamins, and minerals, however, is not very different from that of younger adults.

The elderly should limit their intake of fatty foods, sweets, salty snack foods, high-calorie drinks, and alcohol. These foods contain many calories but few nutrients. Eating them in place of more nutritious foods can lead to weight gain without adequate nourishment.

A nutritious (well-balanced) diet provides vitamins, minerals, and calories from proteins, carbohydrates, and some fats. Such a diet must include a variety of foods from each of the major food groups: fruits and vegetables; whole grain and enriched breads, cereals, and grain products such as rice and pasta; fish, poultry, meats, eggs, and dry peas and beans; and milk, cheese, and other dairy products.

Limiting the amount of fat in the diet may help prevent weight gain. Excess weight is a factor in some disorders that occur in older people, such as diabetes, heart disease, and high blood pressure. Limiting fat in the diet may also help protect against cancer of the breast and colon. Decreasing excessive salt intake is another good health measure.

Some elderly people do not eat enough foods that supply the necessary nutrients. As a result, they may not get the vitamins, minerals, and calories they need to stay healthy and active.

Older people should follow their doctor's advice about eating, especially if they have illnesses that require changes in what or how much they eat, or if they are taking medicine. Some drugs interact with certain foods. Some medicines, too, can affect appetite or change the body's nutritional requirements.

5. SAFE USE OF MEDICINES

Prescription and some over-the-counter drugs can be wonderful tools for the care of patients of all ages. But in older adults drug use may have greater risks, especially when several drugs are taken at one time.

People over 65 make up 11 percent of the American population, yet they consume 25 percent of all prescription drugs sold in this country. As a group, older people tend to have more long-term illnesses—

such as arthritis, diabetes, high blood pressure, and heart disease—than younger people. And because they often have a number of diseases at the same time, it is very common for them to be taking many different drugs.

In general, drugs taken by older people act differently from the way they do in young or middle-aged people. This is probably the result of the normal changes in body makeup that occur with age. For example, as the body grows older, the percent of water and lean tissue (mainly muscle) decreases, while the percent of fat tissue increases. These changes can affect the length of time a drug stays in the body and the amount absorbed by body tissues.

The kidneys and the liver are two important organs responsible for breaking down and removing most drugs from the body. With age, these organs begin to function less efficiently, and thus drugs leave the body more slowly. This may account for the fact that older people tend to have more undesirable reactions to drugs than do younger people.

It is important to remember that "drugs" include not only prescription medicines (those ordered by a doctor and dispensed by a pharmacist) but over-the-counter (OTC) medicines as well (those bought and used without a prescription). Drugs prescribed by a doctor are usually more powerful and have more side effects than OTC medicines. Yet many OTC drugs contain strong agents, and when large quantities are taken, they can equal a dose that would normally only be available by prescription.

Some substances, including vitamins, laxatives, cold remedies, antacids, and alcohol, can also lead to serious problems if used too often or in combination with certain other drugs.

There is much that you and your family can do to reduce the risks of drug use. By learning about the drugs you take and their possible side effects, you can help bring about safer and faster treatment results. Some basic rules for safe drug use are as follows:

- Take exactly the amount of drug prescribed by your doctor and follow the dosage schedule as closely as possible. If you have trouble or questions, call your doctor or pharmacist.
- Medicines do not produce the same effects in all people. Never take drugs prescribed for a friend or relative, even though your symptoms may be the same.
- Always tell your doctor about past problems you have had with drugs (such as rashes, indigestion, dizziness, or lack of appetite). When your doctor prescribes a new drug, be sure to mention all other medicines you are currently taking—including those prescribed by another doctor and those you buy without a prescription.
- Keep a daily record of the drugs you are taking, especially if your treatment schedule is complicated or you are taking more than one drug at a time. The record should show the name of the drug, the doctor who prescribed it, the amount you take, and the times of day for taking it. Include a space to check off each dose as you take it. Keep a copy in your medicine cabinet and one in your wallet or pocketbook.
- If child-proof containers are hard for you to handle, ask your pharmacist for easy-to-open

containers. Always be sure, however, that
they are out of the reach of children.

- Make sure you understand the directions
printed on the drug container and that the
name of the medicine is clearly printed on
the label. Ask your pharmacist to use large
type on the label if you find the regular labels
hard to read.
- Discard old medicines; many drugs lose their
effectiveness over time.
- When you start taking a new drug, ask your
doctor or pharmacist about side effects that
may occur, about special rules for storage,
and about foods or beverages, if any, to avoid.
Remember pharmacists are drug specialists
and are able to answer most questions about
drug use.
- Always call your doctor promptly if you
notice unusual reactions.
- New information about drugs and about how
they affect the older user is coming to light
daily. You should occasionally review with
your doctor the need for each medicine.
- Remember that a chemical agent strong
enough to cure an ailment is also strong
enough to cause harm, if it's not used wisely.
Although you should never stop taking medicines without medical advice, if you feel any
drug is doing more harm than good, don't be
afraid to discuss the matter with your doctor.
He or she may be able to substitute another
medicine that will be effective.

6. ACCIDENTS AND THE ELDERLY

Accidents seldom "just happen." Many can be prevented. Accidental injuries become more frequent and serious in later life. Thus, attention to safety is especially important for older persons.

Several factors make people in this age group prone to accidents. Poor eyesight and hearing can decrease awareness of hazards. Arthritis, neurological diseases, and impaired coordination and balance can make older people unsteady.

Various diseases, medication, alcohol, and preoccupation with personal problems can result in drowsiness or distraction. Often mishaps are expressions of mental depression or of poor physical conditioning.

When accidents occur, older persons are especially vulnerable to severe injury and tend to heal slowly. Particularly in women, the bones often become thin and brittle with age, causing seemingly minor falls to result in broken bones.

Many accidents can be prevented by maintaining mental and physical health and conditioning, and by cultivating good safety habits.

Falls are the most common cause of fatal injury in the aged. Proper lighting can help prevent them. Here's what you can do:

- Illuminate all stairways and provide light switches at both the bottom and the top.
- Provide night lights or bedside remote-control light switches.
- Be sure both sides of stairways have sturdy handrails.
- Tack down carpeting on stairs and use non-skid treads.

- Remove throw rugs that tend to slide.
- Arrange furniture and other objects so they are not obstacles.
- Use grab bars on bathroom walls and non-skid mats or strips in the bathtub.
- Keep outdoor steps and walkways in good repair.

Personal health practices are also important in preventing falls. Because older persons tend to become faint or dizzy when standing too quickly, experts recommend arising slowly from sitting or lying positions. Both illness and the side effects of drugs increase the risk of falls.

Burns are especially disabling in the aged, who recover from such injuries more slowly. Some good practices to follow are:

- Never smoke in bed or when drowsy.
- When cooking, don't wear loosely fitting flammable clothing. Bathrobes, nightgowns, and pajamas can catch fire.
- Set water heater thermostats or faucets so that water does not scald the skin.
- Plan which emergency exits to use in case of fire.

Many older people trap themselves behind multiple door locks which are hard to open during an emergency. Install one good lock that can be opened from the inside quickly, rather than many inexpensive locks.

Motor vehicle accidents are the most common cause of accidental death among the 65-to-75 age group, and the second most common cause among older persons in general. Your ability to drive may be impaired by such age-related changes as increased sensitivity to glare, poor adaptation to dark, diminished coordination, and slower reaction time. You can compensate for these changes by driving fewer miles; driving less often and more slowly; and driving less at night, during rush hours, and in the winter.

If you ride on public transportation:

- Remain alert and brace yourself when a bus is slowing down or turning.
- Watch for slippery pavement and other hazards when entering or leaving a vehicle.
- Have fare ready to prevent losing your balance while fumbling for change.
- Do not carry too many packages, and leave one hand free to grasp railings.
- Allow extra time to cross streets, especially in bad weather.
- At night wear light-colored or fluorescent clothing and carry a flashlight.

Older people constitute about 11 percent of the population and suffer 23 percent of all accidental deaths. The National Safety Council reports that each year about 24,000 persons over age 65 die from accidental injuries and at least 800,000 others sustain injuries severe enough to disable them for at least one day. Attention to safety, especially in later life, can prevent much untimely death and disability.

7. CAN LIFE BE EXTENDED?

Why do people grow old and die? Can anything be done to slow aging or extend life? These questions have been around as long as man himself, but there are still no simple answers.

Each day scientists learn more about changes in the human body as it ages. But why these changes occur is still a mystery. Most scientists believe that aging is a complex process involving many body systems.

What Causes Aging?

There are many theories about why aging and death occur. All of them focus on what happens in the body's cells as time goes by. Changes occur which alter the cells' ability to function. When enough cells are altered, aging changes—and finally death—result.

Some theories of aging suggest that such changes are due to a built-in genetic program. Just as early growth and development follow a set timetable, so do maturity, aging, and death. (The late-life time-table, however, is much more variable than the early-life one.)

Other theories assume that aging is caused by damage that occurs in various body systems through-out life. Such damage could be caused by "wear and tear," harmful substances that we breathe and eat, or natural processes within the body. The "damage" theories hold promise that such changes might someday be corrected or avoided and life expectancies extended. However, they also have opened the way for aging "treatments" that scientists do not endorse.

Proposed "Anti-aging" Treatments

One damage theory says that aging is caused by free radicals. These chemicals are produced naturally in all animals that use oxygen. They bounce around inside body cells, often damaging their membranes and the vital proteins, fats, and DNA (deoxyribonucleic acid) within them.

To protect itself, the body uses "antioxidants," compounds which block much of this free radical damage. Some antioxidants, such as SOD (superoxide dismutase), are produced in the body. Others (vitamins A and C and the minerals zinc and selenium, for example) are gotten from food.

Based on this theory, some people suggest that you can extend your life by taking large amounts of antioxidant supplements. There is no evidence that this will work. The body's needs for antioxidants can be met by eating a variety of nutritious foods. There is no reason to believe that extra amounts will do a better job of fighting freeradicals. Furthermore, taking large doses of some of these vitamins and minerals can be harmful. Oral supplements of antioxidants such as SOD have no effect because they are digested before body cells can use them.

Another theory says that aging results from a slow buildup of damage to the DNA in body cells. DNA directs the machinery of every cell. Eventually, DNA damage would cause cells, then body tissues and organs, to break down and die.

Supplements containing DNA and RNA (ribonucleic acid, which works with DNA in the cell) are being sold to slow aging, cure senility, and treat skin and hair changes. Again, there is no scientific evidence to support such claims. Like SOD, DNA and

RNA preparations are useless because the body cannot absorb them.

According to another theory, changes in body hormones are responsible for aging. At some point, a gland such as the pituitary releases a hormone (or fails to produce one) and aging changes begin.

For example, scientists have shown that a hormone called DHEA (dehydroepiandrosterone) which is produced in the adrenal gland may play a role in aging. Young humans have higher levels of DHEA in their blood than do older ones, and DHEA supplements seem to help laboratory rats stay healthy and live longer.

Because of these findings, a preparation labelled DHEA is being sold as a life extender. However, the tablets contain such small amounts of DHEA that they could not possibly have an effect. Furthermore, DHEA supplements have not been tested in humans. Scientists do not even know if large amounts would affect longevity.

Another theory of aging focuses on the immune system, which is the body's weapon for fighting disease. As people grow older, this system becomes less effective, opening the way for infection by viruses, bacteria, and other disease-producing organisms. As the immune system ages it also tends to lose the ability to tell the difference between the body's own tissues and foreign substances. As a result, cells of the immune system that once would fight invading organisms now attack the body itself, producing disease.

A way to extend life by delaying aging changes in the immune system was proposed recently. The technique involves reducing the amount of food eaten so that a large percentage of body weight is lost over a period of years. Dietary restriction is known to extend the lives of laboratory mice and rats, but there is no evidence that it has this effect in humans.

Scientists are studying the aging theories described above. But even if they discover which one (or ones) is correct, there is no guarantee that a way to extend life will result.

Check with a doctor before buying a supplement or making a dietary change. Be suspicious of any product that promises to slow aging, extend life, or produce major changes in appearance or vigor.

Can Anything Be Done To Extend Life?

There are no known "anti-aging" treatments, drugs, or supplements that slow aging or extend life. But your chances of staying healthy and living a long time will improve if you:

- Don't smoke.
- Eat a balanced diet and maintain your desirable weight.
- Exercise regularly.
- Have regular health checkups, see a doctor when you detect a problem, and follow a doctor's advice when taking medications.
- Stay involved with family and friends.
- Allow time for rest and relaxation.
- Get enough sleep
- Stay active through work, recreation, and community activities.
- Drink alcoholic beverages in moderation, if at all, and don't drive after drinking.
- Use seatbelts when you drive or ride in a car.
- Avoid overexposure to the sun and cold.

- Practice good safety habits at home to prevent accidents such as fires and falls.

It also helps to have a positive attitude toward life. *Expect* to live a long time. Plan ahead for housing and financial security. Find out what makes you happy and do it.

8. HEALTH QUACKERY

We hear a great deal today about the rising cost of health care. But seldom do health care costs reflect the money wasted on medical quackery—the promotion of remedies and devices that are scientifically unproven. Each year American consumers pay roughly $10 billion for ineffective, expensive, and sometimes harmful products.

Also staggering are the indirect costs of health quackery—medical expenses resulting from a delay in legitimate treatment or from injury by a quack "treatment." The indirect cost last year for arthritis fraud alone was about $25 million.

Quacks—those who sell unproven remedies— have been around for many years. You may remember the "snake oil" salesman who traveled from town to town making outrageous claims about a doubtful product. Today's quack is a little more sophisticated. He or she sells products through advertisements, bogus corporations, foundations, and clinics.

Who are the Victims?

To the quack, people of all ages are fair game, but older people form the largest group of victims. So serious is the impact of fraud on the elderly that the

Subcommittee on Health and Long-Term Care, of the U.S. House of Representatives, conducted a four-year investigation on quackery. The committee issued their findings in the report "Quackery: A $10 Billion Scandal" and concluded that 60 percent of all victims of health-care fraud are older persons, although older persons make up 11 percent of the U.S. population.

Most people who succumb to the quack's worthless and sometimes dangerous "treatments" are desperate for some offer of hope. Because older people as a group have more chronic illnesses (arthritis, high blood pressure, diabetes, and cancer) compared to younger people, they are likely targets for medical fraud.

Major Targets of Quackery

Three of the largest areas for health quackery are the aging process, arthritis, and cancer.

Aging—The normal process of aging is a rich territory for medical quackery. In a youth-oriented society, quacks find it easy to promote a wide variety of products simply by saying they can stop or reverse the aging process or relieve conditions associated with old age. Thus, special cosmetics are said to erase wrinkles, vitamins to enhance virility, and creams to reverse baldness. While a healthy lifestyle can help delay many conditions associated with the aging process, no preparation or device on the market can stop aging.

Arthritis—Older persons who suffer from arthritis are another major target for quacks. Arthritis "remedies" are especially easy to fall for because symptoms of arthritis tend to recede or disappear for a period of time for unknown reasons. Persons with arthritis then associate the remedy they happen to be using with relief from symptoms. Arthritis sufferers have paid good money for bottled seawater, "extracts" from New Zealand green-lipped mussels, and Chinese herbal medicines (which have no herbs but do contain drugs that may be dangerous).

There is no cure for most forms of arthritis at the present, but treatments are available through qualified medical sources that can help reduce pain and enable greater movement. These include drugs, heat treatments, a balance of rest and exercise, and in some cases surgical implants.

Cancer—This disease is currently responsible for one-fifth of all deaths in the U.S. and, as with arthritis, cancer occurs more often in older people. Quacks prey on the older person's fear of cancer by offering "treatments" that have no proven value—for example, a vegetarian diet dangerously low in protein or drugs such as Laetrile.

Recent progress made in combatting cancer is enormous; today almost 50 percent of cancer victims survive for at least five years. But this rate might be even higher—if all patients promptly consulted a qualified doctor instead of losing time on worthless remedies!

How to Protect Yourself and Help Stop Quackery

By staying alert to signs of quackery, you and your family can protect yourselves and help stop the spread of medical fraud. One way of doing this is to question carefully what you see or hear in advertisements. Although there are exceptions, the editors of newspapers, magazines, radio, and TV do not regularly screen their ads for truth or accuracy. So be aware that ads for cosmetics and health aids are not necessarily true just because they are presented by what may otherwise be a "reputable" source!

Also, find out about a product before you buy it. Health products sold door-to-door should be checked out first through a local agency such as the Better Business Bureau.

The following are common ploys used by dishonest promoters:

- Promising a quick or painless cure.
- Promoting a product made from a "special" or "secret" formula, usually available through the mail and from only one sponsor.
- Presenting testimonials or case histories from satisfied patients.
- Advertising a product as effective for a wide variety of ailments.
- Claiming to understand the cause or cure for a disease (such as arthritis or cancer) not yet understood by medical science.

If you have questions about what you believe may be a quack product, the most important resource is a qualified physician.

CHAPTER 8

A New Career

CHAPTER 8

A New Career

As you prepare for retirement you may discover that you need or like to work. But remember Part-time or Full-time work has a financial impact on your Social Security income. As of this writing, at the age of 62 you can earn $7,444.00 per year without affecting your social security income, and $10,200.00 per year at the age of 65. When you reach 70 you can earn all the money you want without affecting your social security income.

Work can add structure to your life, especially the kind of work you enjoy! Some retired people use their retirement years to start a business. They feel more secure with an established income, but more important, they have the time. Time allows the retired person to contemplate a new career and use the experience they have gained over the last 40 years or so, and put it to good use. The opportunities are many, consulting, franchising, at-home business of all kinds, real estate sales are some of the popular self-employment options. You must carefully evaluate before launching a business and maybe fulfilling the dream of a lifetime. To start and run a business requires a good idea, lots of work and commitment, money and a good manager. For other retirees however the answer is part-time work in a new career or maybe to continue at their current employer on a part-time basis. Consider that....

- A survey of 10,000 IBM retirees in the mid-1980s reported that 68 percent of all company retirees, and 78 percent of those with recent retirement experiences, said they would like to return to work for the company. Almost all of the respondents expressed interest in part-time employment, most often described as a few days a week (rather than a few hours a day or a few weeks a year).
- A Gallup Poll survey for the American Association of Retired Persons reported that while 53 percent of retirees were happily retired, 29 percent said they would rather be working. In the latter group, close to half noted that they had retired for health reasons or were too old to work.
- A 1981 survey conducted by Louis Harris Associates for the National Council on the Aging indicated that 79 percent of the work force between the ages of 55 and 64 expressed interest in part-time employment rather than retiring completely. A later Harris survey (1986) found that 17 percent of older adults were working either full-time or part-time and an additional 10 percent wanted paying jobs.

There are at least three options you have if you want to continue being part of the working population:

1. Working Part-Time
2. Starting A Business
3. Starting A Business At Home

But whatever you decide you must include your family in any of those options—particularly, if you start a business. You might require your spouse to help and maybe request others to participate.

1. WORKING PART-TIME

Part-time work has many advantages, it will give you some free time to pursue your own interests, hobbies or pleasures. Perhaps your former employer will allow you to work part-time or other local firms in the same field will hire you part-time. Other opportunities are the temporary employment agencies. "Mature Temps" is a employment agency that provides temporary or full-time jobs for older people. Also inform your local Human Resource Department and Chamber of Commerce that you are available for part-time work opportunities. Part-time employment can provide great satisfaction and a sense of belonging to the working environment and some extra income.

2. STARTING A BUSINESS

Starting a business is what most retirees desire. However, the odds are not favorable. The statistics tell us that two out of three business starts will fail within two years. The reasons are:

1. No Financial Strength
2. Partnership Problems
3. Lack of Proper Management

However, there are many success stories of retirees that have done well including Colonel Sanders with "Kentucky Fried Chicken." Success is sweet. A full discussion of establishing a business is not within the scope of this book. However, some publications are listed in the back of this book "Retirement Resources" to familiarize yourself with establishing a business and other useful publications relating to starting a successful enterprise.

3. STARTING A BUSINESS AT HOME

The home business is enjoying a revival so strong that it is difficult to find out just how many Americans are now working at home. Estimates range from two to five million and the numbers might double by 1993. Retired people interested in a second income are one of the groups attracted to home enterprises. A retired government worker bought 36 beehives and sold honey to local health food stores and craft fairs. A retired teacher did typing and secretarial jobs for friends until she realized the potential market and opened a full-time secretarial service from her home. Others have become business owners by using their skills in catering, counseling, teaching, day care, sewing, writing, consulting, and market research. The list of services that have been successfully operated from home is nearly endless. Home business is attractive for several reasons. The cost of doing business is low. You do not have to pay rent to house your business. You do not have to travel from home to work. Operating out of your garage or den is very practical and can be tax deductible.

Nothing comes without risk. It is therefore wise to prepare before you invest your time and money. Successful home-based business owners learn from experience—their own and that of others.

How to Learn From Experience

You can learn from experience in several ways:

First, work closely and creatively with professional advisors, such as your lawyer and accountant. As you continually review your business records, you will see "mistakes," but you will also begin to develop skill in planning and managing.

Second, continue to learn about all areas of business operations, constantly acquiring new ideas. Most community colleges have short, inexpensive, practical courses for business owners in topics like "Financing a Small Business," "Choosing a Small Business Computer," and "Starting and Operating a Home-Based Business."

Third, get to know other business owners with similar needs or problems. Talking with others may be a way to avoid repeating the mistakes they have made and benefiting from their experience. Local and national organizations offer membership, social events, networking opportunities, newsletters, and seminars for home-based business owners. Through these organizations you can often advertise your product or service to other business owners. They also provide a way to learn about services you may need, such as accounting, public relations, or a responsible secretarial service. These organizations offer updates in such areas as taxes and zoning in their newsletters and workshops.

Finding and Using Resources, Networks, and Support Groups

Start out with the attitude: "Whatever my current business problem, I can find the solution."

Somewhere out there is information, a book, a person, an organization, or a government agency that can help. A word of warning though: finding resources and building networks can be very time-consuming. Joining organizations can turn out to be expensive, especially if you are too busy to use their services and support once you join. So use this list to organize your search for resources useful to you, then pick and choose carefully what you decide to read, join, buy, or attend.

Your Public Library: Visit your local library. Get to know all its resources. In addition to books, many libraries offer free workshops, lend skill-building tapes, and catalogues and brochures describing continuing education opportunities for business owners. Ask the librarian for current copies of zoning regulations. Get familiar with new books and resources in your field (computers, health care, crafts, etc.) Look for magazines such as *In Business, Black Enterprise, Venture,* or *The Journal of Small Business Management. Reading selectively is free. Subscribing to too many magazines may be expensive.*

Organizations: A wide variety of local and national organizations have sprung up to serve the informational, lobbying, and networking needs of business entrepreneurs. Through meetings, services, or newsletters, groups such as the National Association of Women Business Owners, American Entrepreneurs Association, Business and Professional Women's Club, National Alliance of Homebased Businesswomen, and the National Association for Cottage Industry offer members everything from camaraderie to valuable "perks," such as group rates on health insurance. David Gumpert's book, *The Insider's Guide to Small Business Resources,* has addresses of many of these groups and other information on such resources.

Government Resources: Contact your local or district office of the U.S. Small Business Administration (SBA) to learn about SBA services and publications. The SBA also offers free or inexpensive workshops and counseling through SCORE.® SCORE® is a volunteer program sponsored by the SBA through which retired executives, who have management expertise, are linked with owners/managers of small business or prospective entrepreneurs who need help.

The Department of Commerce, Bureau of the Census, Department of Defense (procurement), Department of Labor, IRS (ask for the free "Business Tax Kit"), Federal Trade Commission, and the Government Printing Office all have publications and services to inform and support you. Local and state government offices may also have services to help you. Addresses will be available in your telephone book, under the U.S. Government, at your public library, or at the SBA office near you.

Community colleges: Most community colleges now have short, inexpensive, non-credit programs for entrepreneurs. The classes usually are convenient to business owners and are taught by experienced owners and managers.

As a home-based business person you can overcome feelings of isolation and give and receive valuable information if you tap into networks and resources. Being active in professional and trade associations will help to build a good marketing network for your service or product. Take the time and invest the money for memberships. Then continually evaluate which organizations and resources best serve your business information and networking needs.

SOME GOOD ADVICE FOR YOU
AND YOUR HOME BUSINESS

Expect to encounter stress and time problems similar to those of other business owners but accentuated by the fact that you work at home. Follow these guidelines to make it a little easier on yourself:

1) Plan your time and establish priorities on a daily "to do" list. Decide what your "prime time" is and do your most important or difficult tasks then. Set "business hours," specific time when you are at work and times when you turn on the answering machine because you are "on duty but off call." You, your customers, and your family will appreciate knowing your set routine, even though you know that for special events or emergencies you can break that schedule.

2) Notice what your four or five big time-wasters are and learn techniques to eliminate them or compensate for them. Some common ones are: telephone interruptions, visitors, socializing, excessive paperwork, lack of policies and procedures, procrastination, failure to delegate, unclear objectives, poor scheduling, lack of self-discipline, and lack of skill in a needed area.

3) Stay in contact with people. Even though you prefer to work at home, you should plan work-related or social activities that provide frequent contact with others. This will help your morale if you feel isolated. Even for home-based business owners who like feeling isolated, keeping up with business and professional contacts is a must.

4) Build a fitness program into your day.
Many successful entrepreneurs exercise in order to
think creatively because physical activity sends
oxygen to the brain and helps the mind function
better. With regular exercise your health will improve, your stress level will go down, and your trim
look will inspire people to have confidence in your
abilities.

**5) Give your home business as much of a
separate and distinct physical identity as possible.**
Although you might save a few dollars by using the
ironing board as a bookshelf and a cardboard box as
a file cabinet, the stress and strain of operating without proper space and supplies will take its toll. Have a
separate room or area for your business, with a separate entrance if customers or suppliers visit. Consider
soundproofing so your family won't be bothered by
your noise and vice versa. (In addition to the psychological and physical comfort of having a separate
office, the IRS requires it in order for you to make a
legitimate claim for tax deductions.)

**6) Take care of your major business asset:
YOU.** Being the boss can be exciting, fulfilling, and
rewarding. It can also be lonely, stressful, and de-
manding. Learn to balance your professional and
personal life. Go on vacation. Get a weekly massage.
Join a health club. Take a class in meditation. Attend
a business owner's breakfast club. Your business
depends on you to be at your best.
Finally...remember, you are retired. If you plan
to launch a business or enter into a part-time or full-
time job make your retirement years fun. This is a
time of choice, make it the best years of your life.

CHAPTER 9

Conclusion

CHAPTER 9

Conclusion

There is a notion among people that it is easy to retire. This is not true. The change from an active life to a leisure one is a dramatic occurrence. Most of your working life you have been paid and rewarded for your efforts as an employee. You have enjoyed the companionship of your co-workers and shared their daily activities. It has been a lifestyle that occupied your time at least five days a week, your social life was often connected with that. In addition, you planned a two weeks well deserved vacation during the year. Then this busy schedule of 52 weeks has come a sudden halt. A major change in your lifestyle! It is therefore wise not to treat your retirement years as a vacation. Vacation is a break from what you are doing. Soon, boredom will set in followed by depression, and you will begin to miss your active work schedule. Stay active; start building a new life. Be in control of your retirement, prepare and make decisions for the future. Search for your needs and plan it. Personally contribute more to the retirement years than just your income. Your ability to maintain health and good spirits will determine your longevity. The knowledge about physical, emotional and practical aspects of aging and the chances to live to a ripe-old-age is greater than ever. But preparation is essential for a successful retirement. Standing on the threshold of your retirement, you can look forward to a 20 to 25 years of new opportunities. You have more time and freedom, you can go where you want and when you want. You can draw on what you have learned and plan a brand new tomorrow. This situation has never presented itself this way in your life. You probably feel much younger in your heart than the calendar tells you. Use that energy to motivate yourself to a new beginning.

I hope this book has raised your level of awareness and provided you with the basic needs on which you can build a happy retirement. The well known comedian George Burns (96) said: "Keep working as long as you can. Remember, you can't help getting older, but you don't have to get old.... There's an old saying, 'Life begins at 40.' That's silly—life begins every morning when you wake up. Open your mind to it; don't just sit there—do things!"

I hope I've helped you plan intelligently for your retirement. Proper planning will reap rewards and can make these years "the golden years of your life."

HAPPY RETIREMENT

CHAPTER 10

Retirement Sources

CHAPTER 1 — INTRODUCTION

National Association of Area Agencies on Aging
Suite 208 W
600 Maryland Avenue S.W.
Washington, DC 20024
(202) 484-7520

The National Association of Area Agencies on Aging
(NAAAA) represents the interests of approximately 650
Area Agencies on Aging across the country.

American Association of Retired Persons
1909 K Street N.W.
Washington, DC 20029
(202) 872-4700

The American Association of Retired Persons (AARP) is
an consumer organization that seeks to improve the
quality of life for older people.

American Society on Aging
Suite 512
833 Market Street
San Francisco, CA 94103
(415) 543-2617

The American Society on Aging is a nonprofit, membership organization that informs the public and health
professionals about issues that affect the quality of life
for older persons and promotes innovative approaches
to meeting the needs of these individuals.

GOVERNMENT AGENCIES AND PUBLICATIONS

Consumer Information Center
Pueblo, CO 81009

Good source for government publications, including many on various aspects of retirement; many are free. A catalog of publications is available free from Department A of the center.

Gray Panthers (National Office)
3700 Chestnut Street
Philadelphia, PA 19104

American Association of Retired Persons and National Retired Teachers Association
1909 K Street Northwest
Washington, DC 20049

An organization that provides many beneficial information for retired people, including insurance, travel and health.

CHAPTER 2 — SOME INTERESTING STATISTICS

National Center for Health Statistics
3700 East-West Highway
Hyattsville, MD 20872
(301) 436-8500

The National Center for Health Statistics (NCHS), part of the Public Health Service, collects, analyzes, and distributes data on health in the United States.

U.S. Department of Commerce
Bureau of Statistics
Customer Services
Data User Services Division
Washington, DC 20233
(301) 763-4100

CHAPTER 3 — BASIC PLANNING

American Association of Retired Persons
1909 K Street N.W.
Washington, DC 20049
(202) 872-4700

A source for materials concerning: A Guide To Long Term Care Choices, and Other Planning Programs.

Government Printing Office
Government publications:
Publications Service Section
Government Printing Office
Washington, DC 20402
(202) 275-3050

Good source for government publications relating to planning. Many booklets are free.

CHAPTER 4 — YOUR SOCIAL
SECURITY BENEFITS

Social Security Administration
Office of Public Inquiries
6401 Security Boulevard
Baltimore, MD 21235
(301) 594-1234

The Social Security Administration is the Federal Government agency responsible for the Social Security retirement, survivors, and disability program, as well as the Supplemental Security Income program.

Also, look in your local telephone directory under U.S. Government, Health and Human Services Department, Social Security Administrations.

Department of Health and Human Services
The following departments are sources for information and guidance.

Consumer Affairs and Information Staff
Food & Drug Administration (HFC-110)
Department of Health and Human Services
5600 Fishers Lane, Room 13-86
Rockville, MD 20857
(301)443-4166

National Health Information Center
Department of Health and Human Services
P.O. Box 113
Washington, DC 20013
(202) 429-9091
1-800-336-4797 (toll free)

Health Care Financing Administration
Department of Health and Human Services
6325 Security Boulevard
Baltimore, MD 21207
(301) 594-9086

Health Insurance Association of America
Suite 1200
1025 Connecticut Ave. N.W.
Washington, DC 20036
(202) 223-7780
Information Service
1 800-423-8000 (toll free)

The Health Insurance Association of America offers information to the public about all aspects of health and disability insurance. The toll free information service provides information about health insurance companies in the United States and answers general questions about insurance coverage, including questions about supplementary Medicare insurance. (Specific inquires about individual insurance policies, however, must be directed to the appropriate insurance company.)

Cancer Hotline
1-800-4-CANCER (toll free in continental U.S.)
1-800-638-6070 (toll free in Alaska)
1-800-524-1234 (Hawaii)

CHAPTER 5 — STAYING OR MOVING

National Council on the Aging
West Wing 100
600 Maryland Avenue S.W.
Washington, DC 20024
(202) 479-1200

The National Council on the Aging (NCOA), a non-profit, membership organization for professionals and volunteers, serves as a national resource for information, technical assistance, training, and research relating to the field of aging.

For information on Homes or Apartments, contact National Recognized Real Estate Organizations.

Department of Housing and Urban Development
Contact the following agencies for information and guidance.

Manufactured Housing and Construction Standards Div.
Dept. of Housing and Urban Development
Room 9156
Washington, DC 20410
(202) 755-6920

Office of Fair Housing and Equal Opportunity
Dept. of Housing and Urban Development
Room 5100
Washington, DC 20410
(202) 755-7252
1-800-424-8590 (toll free)

Office of Single Family Housing
Dept. of Housing and Urban DevelopmentRoom 9266
Washington, DC 20410
(202) 755-3046

Office of Urban Rehabilitation
Dept. of Housing and Urban Development
Room 7168
Washington, DC 20410
(202) 755-5685

Title I Insurance Division
Dept. of Housing and Urban Development
Room 9160
Washington, DC 20410
(202) 755-6680

American Association of Homes for the Aging
Suite 400
1129 20th Street N.W.
Washington, DC 20036-3489
(202) 296-5960

The American Association of Homes for the Aging
(AAHA) is a professional organization of nonprofit
nursing homes, independent housing facilities, continuing care communities, and community service
agencies.

Services
- It helps members meet the social, health, and
  environmental needs of the individuals they
  serve, plus the Association offers a number of
  continuing education programs.

- The Association encourages community involvement in nursing homes to ensure the highest quality of care for residents.
- The Associations reviews and accredits/ certifies continuing care communities.
- The Association provides free information on long-term care and housing for older people (including information about Association-approved housing programs) to the public.

It is also recommended to rent or swap housing before you make a permanent move. The following organizations will assist you finding contacts.

Interchange Home Exchange
P.O. Box 3975
San Francisco, CA 94119

Inter Service Home Exchange
P.O. Box 87
Glen Echo, MD 20812

Holiday Home Exchange Bureau
P.O. Box 878
Belen, MN 87002

ECHO Housing
Coastal Colonial Corporation
Box 452-A, R.D. 4
Manheim, PA 17545

ECHO Housing can provide self contained cottages designed for retired people to maintain their independence.

CHAPTER 6 — RETIREMENT AND THE LAW

National Council of Senior Citizens
925 15th Street N.W.
Washington, DC 20005
(202) 347-8800

The National Council of Senior Citizens, a nonprofit
association of clubs, councils, and other community
groups, works as an advocate on behalf of older Americans.

National Senior Citizens Law Center
Suite 400
2025 M. Street N.W.
Washington, DC 20036
(202) 887-5280

The National Senior Citizens Law Center (NSCLC) is a
public interest law firm that specializes in the legal
problems of older people.

National Consumers League
815 15th Street N.W., Ste. 516
Washington, DC 20005
(202) 639-8140

The National Consumers League is a private, nonprofit
group that works to educate consumers and to bring
consumer concerns to the attention of government and
industry decision makers.

Legal Services for the Elderly
132 W. 43rd Street, 3rd Fl.
New York, NY 10036
(212) 391-0120

Legal Services for the Elderly (LSE) is an advisory center for lawyers who specialize in the legal problems of older persons.

American Bar Association Commission on the Legal Problems of the Elderly
Second Floor, South Lobby
1800 M Street N.W.
Washington, DC 20036
(202) 331-2297

The Commission on the Legal Problems of the Elderly, a program of the American Bar Association, analyzes and responds to the legal needs of older people in the United States.

The Commission supports community agencies that provide low-cost legal services to older persons and offer educational programs to the public on legal issues of special interest to older adults and their families.

Alliance Against Fraud in Telemarketing
c/o National Consumers League
815 15th Street N.W., Suite 516
Washington, DC 20005
(202) 639-8140

CHAPTER 7 — STAY ACTIVE AND HEALTHY

President's Council on Physical Fitness and Sports
450 Fifth St. N.W., Suite 7103
Washington, DC 20001
(202) 272-3430

The President's Council on Physical Fitness and Sports (PCPFS) encourages Americans to raise their fitness levels.

Services
• The Council distributes information to the public about the health-related benefits of regular exercise.

Senior Sports International Association
5225 Wilshire Boulevard, Ste. 302
Los Angeles, CA 90036

American Association of Fitness Directors in Business and Industry
P.O. Box 2000
Leesburg, VA 22073

Information on Health and Fitness
Center for Science in the Public Interest
1501 16th Street N.W.
Washington, DC 20036

Provides materials on proper nutrition and fitness.

Organizations for special health problems

Arthritis Foundation
1314 Spring Street N.W.
Atlanta, CA 30309
(404) 872-7100

National Osteoporosis Foundation
1625 Eye Street N.W.
Washington, DC 20006
(202) 223-2226

Alzheimer's Disease and Related Disorders Assoc., Inc.
360 North Michigan Avenue
Chicago, IL 60601

National Kidney Foundation
2 Park Avenue
New York, NY 10003
(212) 889-2210

National Mental Health Association
1021 Prince Street
Alexandria, VA 22314
(703) 604-7722

American Podiatry Association
20 Chevy Chase Circle NW
Washington, DC 20015

The American Foundation for the Blind
15 West 16th Street
New York, NY 10011

The American Heart Association
7320 Greenville Avenue
Dallas, TX 75231

The American Cancer Society
777 Third Avenue
New York, NY 10017

American Dental Association
211 East Chicago Ave.
Chicago, IL 60611

Self Help for Hard of Hearing People (SHHH)
7800 Wisconsin Avenue
Bethesda, MD 20814
(301) 657-2248

CHAPTER 8 — A NEW CAREER

Equal Employment Opportunity Commission
1801 L Street NW
Washington, DC 20507
(202) 634-6036
Information Service
1-800-872-3362 (toll free)

The Equal Employment Opportunity Commission (EEOC) is the federal agency responsible for eliminating discrimination based on race, color, religion, sex, national origin, age, or disability in hiring, promoting, firing, and all other conditions of employment.

The EEOC enforces the Age Discrimination in Employment Acts, which prohibit employment discrimination against workers or applicants over 40 years of age.

Elderhostel
80 Boylston Street, ste. 400
Boston, MA 02116
(617) 426-8056

Elderhostel is a nonprofit organization that sponsors educational programs for persons 60 years of age and older.

The following organizations can provide information on careers and help retired people with possible work opportunities.

Mature Temps (14 offices nationwide)
1750 K Street N.W.
Washington, DC 20006

New Career Opportunities, Inc.
625 N. Maryland Ave., Rm 207
Glendale, CA 91206

Second Careers Program
611 South Oxford Street
Los Angeles, CA 90005

Work in America Institute
700 White Plains Road
Scarsdale, NY 10583

The National Executive Service Corps
622 Third Avenue
New York, NY 10017

The International Executive Service Corps
622 Third Avenue
New York, NY 10017

The Center for Entrepreneurial Management
311 Main Street
Worcester, MA 01608

Green Thumb, Inc.
1012 14th Street NW
Washington, DC 20005

National Council of Senior Citizens
1511 K Street NW
Washington, DC 20036

National Council on the Aging
1828 L Street NW
Washington, DC 20036

U.S. Small Business Administration
1441 L Street NW
Washington, DC 20549

Institute of Lifetime Learning
1346 Connecticut Avenue NW
Washington, DC 20036

GENERAL

Volunteers of America
3813 North Causeway Boulevard
Metairie, LA 70002
(504) 837-2652

Volunteers of America (VOA) is a nonprofit organization that offers programs and services to meet the specific needs of a local community. Social services are provided to young people, older persons, families, persons with disabilities, alcoholics, and others.

ACTION
1100 Vermont Avenue NW
Washington, DC 20525
(202) 634-9380

ACTION is an agency of the Federal Government that sponsors a number of volunteer programs conducted by older adults.

Action for Independent Maturity (AIM)
1909 K Street NW
Washington, DC 20049

Aim will provide information about money management, health, and many other subjects to streamline your retirement years.

Credit Counseling
National Foundation for Consumer Credit
8701 Georgia Avenue
Silver Spring, MD 20910

This organization can provide direction for people who have problems with paying of loans.

READING MATERIAL

To maintain a keen interest in what is going on in your retirement community, it is a good idea to subscribe to some of the periodicals. These magazines provide information on vacation, health, housing, insurance etc. Some of them discuss current social and political issues. Write for an initial free copy.

MAGAZINES

50 Plus
850 Third Ave.
New York, NY 10017

An independent magazine for the over 50 population.

Senior World
P.O. Box 1565
El Cajon, CA 92022

"Senior World" is a monthly newspaper dedicated to inform, serve and entertain active older adults.

New Choices
28 West 23rd Street
New York, NY 10010

Published by "Reader's Digest"

Golden Years Magazine
P.O. Box 537
Melbourne, FL 32902-0537

A general interest magazine including travel, real estate and health.

Prime Time
Box 391
5910 Mineral Point Rd.
Madison, WI 53701

A general interest magazine originally published for members of the National Association of Retired Credit Union People. Non-member can subscribe as well.

Modern Maturity
American Association of Retired Persons
1909 K Street NW
Washington, DC 20049

This magazine is the official publication of AARP. Your $5.00 membership fee includes the magazine. An excellent publication.

NEWSLETTERS

Mature Outlook Newsletter
6001 N. Clark Street
Chicago, IL 60660-9977

An interesting publication issued 6 times a year with very helpful advice.

Vital Connections
Foundation of Grandparenting
P.O. Box 97
Jay, NY 12941

A newsletter published by Foundation for Grandparenting. A yearly membership will provide you with this newsletter.

The Mature Traveler
Gem Publishing
P.O. Box 50820
Reno, NV 89513

A monthly newsletter that provides you with travel tips and advice on saving cost.

The Retirement Letter
Peter a Dickinson, Editor
44 Wildwood Dr.
Prescott, AZ 86301

A monthly letter that provides financial information after retirement.

BOOKS

Places Rated Almanac
Written by: Richard Boyer & David Savageau
Published by: Prentice Hall New York

An excellent publication on finding a place to live. A guide to look for the best places to live in America. The author ranks 333 metropolitan areas by living cost, job outlook, crime, health, transportation, education, the arts, recreation and climate.

The Complete Retirement Planning Book
Written by: Peter A. Dickinson
Published by: E.P. Dutton, Inc.
                        2 Park Avenue
                        New York, NY 10016

An indispensable classic source book for your retirement years.

The Best Years Book
Written by: Hugh Downs & Richard Roll
Published by: Dell, New York

INDEX

Notes...

Notes...

Notes...

Mr. Krane, educated in the Netherlands, is a successful businessman and has been associated with national and international corporations. He has traveled extensively and interviewed men and women prior to and after retirement. Mr. Krane has a deep understanding of the importance of planning your retirement and to "Get Ready". Author of business-oriented publications he developed the successful program in this book that has helped men and women to make the most of their retirement.

Mr. Krane resides in San Juan Capistrano, California.

ORDER FORM

Please send me _____copies of
Can I Afford Retirement? @ $19.95 per copy _____

California residents include 7-3/4% sales tax _____

Shipping and Handling _____
(Add $1.75 for first book and
75¢ for each additional book)

Total Enclosed _____

Please send check or money order

Ship to:

Name _____

Address _____

City _____ State _____ Zip_____

Allow three to four weeks for delivery

Mail order form to:

**New Leaf Communication
P. O. Box 101
San Juan Capistrano, CA 92693**